ROOKIE COP

ROOKIE
COP

DEEP UNDERCOVER IN THE
JEWISH DEFENSE LEAGUE

by Richard Rosenthal

Leapfrog Press · Wellfleet, Massachusetts

Rookie Cop: Deep Undercover in the Jewish Defense League
Copyright © 2000 Richard Rosenthal

ISBN 0-9654578-8-5

Library of Congress Cataloging-in-Publication Data
Rosenthal, Richard, 1945–
    Rookie cop : deep undercover in the Jewish Defense League / by Richard Rosenthal.
    p. cm.
    ISBN 0-9654578-8-5 (pbk.)
    1. Jewish Defense League. 2. Rosenthal, Richard, 1945– . 3. Undercover operations—New York (State)—New York. 4. Police—New York (State)—New York—Biography. 5. Jews—New York (State)—New York—Biography.
I. Title.
HS2227.J49 R67 2000
363.25'2–dc21   00-025286

First printing August 2000

Printed in the United States

10 9 8 7 6 5 4 3 2 1

The Leapfrog Press
P.O. Box 1495
95 Commercial Street
Wellfleet, MA 02667-1495, USA
www.leapfrogpress.com

Distributed in the United States by
Consortium Book Sales and Distribution
St. Paul, Minnesota 55114
www.cbsd.com

This book is dedicated to Detective William T. Gorman, who passed away less than a year after I surfaced. Bill conducted my initial interviews for acceptance into BOSSI and was the person I reported to early on in the investigation. He was a fine gentleman and a dedicated police officer who died too soon.

CONTENTS

CHAPTER ONE

JOINING THE FORCE

Sol Hurok immigrated to the United States from the village of Pogar, Russia in 1906 and made a small living for himself by producing concerts for New York City's ever growing number of labor societies. Over the years, the workers' craving for highbrow entertainment grew to such an extent that his concerts were staged in the Hippodrome, an enormous amusement hall built by P.T. Barnum. Hurok became the personal manager of the great Afro-American contralto Marian Anderson and arranged the first U.S. tour for the young violin sensation and son of a poor Israeli barber, Itzak Perlman. Within several generations, Hurok became known as The Impresario, importing cultural institutions such as the Comédie Française and the Old Vic to perform for American audiences. A more beneficial, or benign profession would be hard to imagine. Except that the talent he imported also included the Bolshoi Ballet and the Moiseyev Dance Company and there were those who wished to disrupt the ties between the United States and the then-Soviet Union — by any means necessary.

Hurok had been warned many times that he was to stop bringing in Soviet performers. Bottles of ammonia had been uncorked during a number of his events as well as during shows produced by Columbia Artists, a rival company that also imported Russian talent. Live mice and stink bombs had been used to cause upset to the audiences. Some performances had been disrupted by shouting. Annoying as those actions might have been, they hadn't proven effective enough. It was thought that perhaps smoke bombs, delivered right to Hurok's office, as well as those of Columbia Artists, would make the point.

A young man was given some money to buy the chemicals (hypnole and an oxygenator) in order to produce the devices. Although an effective smoke bomb needed only a few ounces of the two materials when combined, he purchased a hundred pounds of the stuff, the reasoning being, if a little smoke was good, a lot of smoke would be better. Then he and another fellow made up two bombs, each weighing thirteen pounds and placed them inside two cheap attaché cases, a small fuse jutting inconspicuously outside each, ready for the match.

Because the members of the group who came up with this idea were either on probation or facing serious criminal charges from recent arrests, it was decided that four fresh faces would be used to plant the two devices. Two teams of high-school age youngsters were to be sent out with the packages; one pair to Columbia Artists, the other to Hurok's. They first met at their headquarters in Brooklyn. There they were shown how to light the fuses and told where to deliver the smoke bombs. The teams then got into one of the young men's cars and headed into Manhattan.

The first device was set off at the Columbia Artists office at 9 A.M. As it was still early in the day, only a handful of employees had arrived at work. When the device went off at the office's entrance, those inside were able to safely escape via a rear exit. No one was injured. It was about 9:30 A.M. when the pair assigned to Hurok's office at Sixth Avenue and Fifty-sixth Street got off the elevator at the twentieth floor. One of the young men went up to a receptionist and inquired about purchasing tickets for some future performance. While the receptionist was busy searching out the information, the two teen-agers placed the attaché case under a table, lit the fuse and quickly departed.

A moment later, one of Hurok's employees noticed smoke coming from across the room. Surprised, he began to rise from his seat when suddenly that part of the room became engulfed in an intense red, pink, and purple flare. He ran from the room. A fraction of a second later, the ignited chemicals began an incendiary fire whose temperature reached 1,700 degrees Fahrenheit. The heat was so intense that lethal chemical reactions took place. Phosgene gas was released from the plastic covering of the blazing furniture. A gas that had proven deadly on the battlefields of World War I would prove equally effective here.

Unlike Columbia Artists, there was no rear exit at Hurok's. The reception area was an inferno, those inside, prisoners. The poison fume spread at a leisurely pace as it made for its victims. Some attempted to fight back, tossing waste buckets of water into the fire. But, at 1,700 degrees water ignites. The people retreated. Behind them, metal objects began to melt. With nowhere to run, workers began smashing panes of glass, letting in fresh air. This act saved their lives. Others found themselves trapped in less fortunate circumstances.

Three women, including twenty-seven year old Iris Kones, took refuge in an inner office. Tendrils of black smoke soon spread under the door. The small space quickly filled with the poison and the three lost consciousness. It took some time for rescuing firemen to locate the three women. Oxygen revived two. But not Kones. She was dead.

Before those responsible were aware they had killed a young Jewish woman, one of those in charge of the operation had already made the obligatory call to the media, saying, "This culture destroys millions of Jews. Cultural bridges of friendship will not be built over the bodies of Soviet Jews. NEVER AGAIN!"

At first, the New York City police department had nothing but a very strong hunch about those responsible for the bombing. The motive, the tactics, and the phone message all pointed to a small group of extremists who were almost unknown when I had been assigned to infiltrate them two years earlier and they had been described to me, in a sadly ironic phrase, as a black cloud on the horizon.

On October 23, 1969, one day before I was to be sworn in as a New York City police officer, I received a call from a man I'd never spoken to before.

"Hi? Dick?"

There were only three people in the world who had ever addressed me as Dick.

"This is Larry. Tomorrow, 11 A.M., be on the southeast corner of Fifty-first Street and Madison Avenue, okay?"

"Are you from . . ."

"Someone will meet you there. Okay, Dick?"

"Sure."

That was it. I really had no idea who Larry worked for or who these people were, although I had been meeting with them for the last few months. And now, I began to really wonder exactly what I was getting myself into. I gave my father the scant information I had as to where I would be going the next day, just in case.

For as long as I can remember I had wanted to be a police officer. It was a desire that had not been looked upon kindly by my parents. The family had its American roots in New York City. Members from my dad's side had arrived in this country before the turn of the century. My mother's father had come over as a child, his people fleeing some Eastern European pogrom. A pogrom, for those unfamiliar with the word, was sort of like a lynching, except the butchers did in entire towns rather than mere individuals. In current English, the term 'ethnic cleansing' comes closest to the word's meaning.

Assimilation into the American culture came quickly. My dad's father served in the Navy during the First World War; my mom's fought in the trenches as a doughboy. His discharge, dated June 10, 1919, indicates that he saw action in the Aisne defensive, the Somme (defensive and offensive), Champagne, the Marne, plus a number of other battles the names of which I cannot make out because of the writer's handwriting. The document further indicates that my grandfather was entitled to a sixty-dollar bonus, *Auth. Act of Congress, Feb. 24, 1919.* Both young men came out of the conflict in one piece, raised families, and slowly moved up the economic ladder into America's theoretically ubiquitous middle class. The quality of life they lived then, and for those members of the family who now remain, would have been unthinkable had it not been for the opportunities this country allowed them to pursue. The goal that children in my family aspired to, what was expected of them, was to attend and graduate from college. But school was dull and boring, and held no attraction for me. What could be more of a rush than to be a cop, particularly with the New York City police department?

I tried my hand at college after high school — and lasted one semester. From there I put in a four-year hitch with the Air Force, where I served in its intelligence arm as a Russian language specialist. After discharge, I succumbed to the pressure of my family's expectations and enrolled in a local college. At that time my folks had left their apartment in Brooklyn and gone over to New Jersey, a move made necessary because of my father's job requirements. But my old dreams of being a police officer were as strong as ever. Half way through the school year, it was February of 1969, I took the written test for the NYPD. I passed the exam, fortunately well up near the top of the list, and was called in to the city, along with several hundred other hopeful applicants, in order to fill out some preliminary paperwork. I remember feeling proud, looking at all the other candidates around me, thinking that I'd soon become part of this special police department.

It wasn't long after that, however, that I received a strange phone call. The gentleman asked if I was still interested in being in the police department. He inquired as to exactly how many people I had mentioned my desire to be a police officer. And finally, he asked me if I could come in for an interview the following Saturday, at the police academy on East Twentieth and First Avenue. The caller's final words were, "And, Dick, don't tell anyone about any of this, okay?"

I was confused and somewhat concerned over the conversation. It just didn't seem quite right. Why the peculiarly worded questions? Why the secrecy? What was I getting myself into?

Showing up a few minutes early for my interview, I entered the police academy and soon realized that the building was empty — deserted, except for a small security staff assigned there during the weekend. I took an elevator up to the appropriate floor and walked down the desolate corridor until coming to the one room that had its lights on. Inside, standing at the opposite side of a gray metal desk, was a neatly dressed, light complexioned man; a beefy fellow, about my size. Detective Bill Gorman put out his hand. "Glad to meet you, Dick. Have a seat." As I complied, I thought to myself that this somewhat florid faced, soft-spoken individual looked and sounded more like a bank manager than a police detective. None of my friends, and no one in my family had ever used this nickname when addressing me. I'd get used to it, however, as Bill and the other detectives I'd soon be working with would rarely call me anything else.

Our meeting began what would be a series of half a dozen such interviews, always at odd hours, in one deserted office or another. It seemed to me that Bill wanted to know my views of the world, my family background, why I wanted to become a police officer. His questions weren't difficult, nor did they seem designed to trip me up; he simply appeared to have a desire to get a sense of me and what I was all about. The meetings went smoothly. Nonetheless, as each was held in a vacant office at an unusual time, it soon became clear to me what I was getting into. Since there was no real direction to our conversation (none that I could see, at any rate), I didn't know how I was doing until, after our third or fourth session, Bill asked, "Who knows you took the police test, Dick?"

"My parents, a few relatives, some friends."

"Tell them you decided not to join the force, that you've changed your mind."

This presented me with a bit of a conflict. I was proud as a peacock that I was soon to be a New York City police officer but now had been told to announce to the world that it wasn't going to happen. Suddenly, an article I had read two years earlier but hadn't thought about since ran through my mind. While in the Air Force I had been assigned to military intelligence and had just finished my day's work of intercepting the chatter of Soviet pilots and their ground controllers. My adversaries, mostly young men my age, were located not very far to the east of where I sat, at Tempelhof Airport in Berlin, West Germany. Even with our powerful array of antennas we were generally only able to hear the pilots responding or reporting to their ground controllers. Often it was just one *Ponyal* (roger) after another. Finished with my evening meal in the mess hall, I wandered into our small airmen's lounge. It had only been twenty years since the end of World War II and U.S. Air Force personnel still occupied a goodly portion of what was formerly an enemy military base but which now served as West Berlin's primary civilian airport. I spotted a copy of *The New York Times* on a coffee table. Picking up the paper, I thumbed through it until one particular article caught my eye. It was about an intelligence gathering organization within the New York City police department. Named the Bureau of Special Service and Investigation, BOSSI, its activities had the *Times* reporter concerned over the police department's use of undercover operatives against other citizens. According to the article, BOSSI (actually the police unit had had a number of different names over the years, BOSSI being the then current iteration) had been around since the beginning of the century. Shortly after it had been formed, a lieutenant from the unit (known as the Red Squad in those days) had been murdered in Italy by members of the Mafia. *The Times* article went on about other places and operations BOSSI had been involved in. I thought to myself, "What a fascinating job that must be: to be an intelligence operative within the New York City police department."

Detective Gorman repeated his question. "Dick, can you do that? Tell your relatives and friends that you've changed your mind about becoming a police officer?"

His words put the pieces of the puzzle together.

"Yes, sure, I can do that," I assured him, shook his hand and went home, not knowing what would be happening next.

Sometime around September I had my final interview. Again it was arranged to take place in the empty police academy building. This time, instead of Bill there were two other men present. Both wore conservative suits. The taller of the two, a thin, almost gaunt man, with sparse graying hair and a complexion as pale as Bill's, introduced himself as Lou. Although he didn't fully identify himself at the time, he was Lieutenant Barnie Mulligan, the man in charge of the undercover section of BOSSI. His was an extraordinarily important position in perhaps one of the most sensitive law enforcement units in the nation, not that I was aware of such things at that moment.

After some initial talk, Lou (he was never referred to as anything else within range of my hearing) asked if I would be interested in volunteering for an undercover police assignment. He went on to explain that the hours would be odd ones, the work possibly dangerous.

At that point, just to show off, I came close to asking him if the unit I would be going into was BOSSI. But for once in my young life, I managed to keep my mouth shut. It was a good thing I did. Some months later, when I told Lou that I had been aware of the existence of BOSSI from that earlier *New York Times* article, he told me he'd never have brought me into the unit had I mentioned my knowledge of its existence.

The next few weeks went by very slowly. I was scheduled to be sworn in as a New York City police officer on October 24, 1969. Two weeks before that date I married Frauke, a young German woman I had met while in Berlin. An architectural engineer by training, she had gone to work in Canada after I left the service, something she'd been planning to do for some time. During that year, I had visited with her up in Toronto and she had come down to my parents home in New Jersey. Although I had asked her to marry me in February, I decided not to tell my parents until a month before the date we'd set. I wasn't being difficult. I simply did not wish to have a "big wedding." I don't like fusses in general. A wedding, with all the attendant planning and the craziness which surrounds such an event seemed like little more than an annoyance to me. Frauke, herself quite reserved, didn't complain. One issue which should be mentioned is the fact that my bride-to-be was not only a native German, but she was not Jewish. I didn't care; Frauke didn't care; more importantly, we didn't care what anyone, either in or out of the family thought about the matter anyway. To us, that negated the issue as any sort of a problem. And, in truth, it never has been. At least not in my family; nor in Frauke's immediate family that I am aware of. Times change. As I am writing this, on my right, tacked up on a cork board in my office, are two pairs of dog tags from my dad's father: one issued to him by the Navy during World War I, and one from the Coast Guard, where he served as a reserve officer during the Second World War while his two sons were in the Army. Next to those is a metal plate on which is affixed the photo of my mother's father wearing his World War I doughboy uniform. And next to that is an Iron Cross, won by my wife's father who was a lieutenant in the German army during the Second World War and served in Italy. It was given to me by my mother-in-law. The medal is not significant to me; the fact that my mother-in-law gave it to me is.

At any rate, my mother, undaunted by the lack of notice, managed to rise to the occasion. The wedding was held at my parent's New Jersey home, which had a fairly large and open backyard. Luck was with us. The weather was perfect on that October day. Mom still managed to invite one hundred and twenty guests. In hindsight, I'm glad I hadn't given her two months notice.

Surreal. That's the only suitable word to describe my first day as a police officer. As directed a day earlier by Larry, I stood on the corner of Fifty-first Street. For the occasion, and as I had for all my meetings with these strange men during the previous months, I wore a conservative suit. While waiting for my contact, I played a little game: try to spot my man before he came up to me. I succeeded. On the opposite side of the street, among the throngs of busy

New Yorkers, a neatly dressed gentleman patiently waited for the light to change. I wasn't surprised when he crossed the street, walked over and said, "Hi, Dick."

"Larry?"

"Just follow about ten feet or so behind me, okay?"

We walked back from the direction Detective Larry McQuade had come, I dutifully keeping ten paces behind the smaller man. We went little more than half a block, dodging and weaving between the flow of pedestrian midday traffic. Larry turned into the entrance of a modest hotel. Ignoring each other, we stood among several other hotel guests waiting for an elevator. The door opened, the small group entered, and on some floor whose number I've long forgotten, both Larry and I got out. Making a sharp right, I stayed on Larry's tail until he came to a room. He knocked, someone opened the door a crack, and the both of us were quickly ushered inside.

Whatever the allotted budget was for hotel rooms permitted my new unit, the sum must have been small. The room was tiny, yet the place was shoulder to shoulder with large men. Introductions were tossed about, men's names blurred in and out of my recall. Except for one, that of detective Teddy Theologes who had been assigned to be my mentor for the next few contacts I'd have with BOSSI personnel.

A thin intense man, I guessed him to be about fifteen years older than me, Teddy, then and always, wore both a suit and, when not indoors and sometimes even then, a gray felt hat. The detective took me off to one side, sat me down, and began reading from a stack of four by six inch index cards. He quickly read off a litany of things a brand new police officer (or, at any rate, one who would very soon be a police officer) working deep undercover had to know. Rates of pay, how to report sick, how I was to be paid (in cash), what would happen to my vacation time (it would be saved for me), when promotion exams were given, how taxes would be handled, and what would happen should the IRS charge any penalties against me (the department would pay them). The list of minutiae went on. It was a complicated thing, being someone else. In fact, to this day my Social Security records are a confused amalgam of two numbers, one gotten for me by the department while I served undercover.

I glanced at the cards in his hands. They had been well used, their edges worn and frayed, and held handwriting so small that I wondered how Teddy managed to read what was on them.

Finally, he informed me I was to go to lunch (as if I was hungry), and then to be on the corner of Court and Broome Streets at 2 P.M. He gave me twenty dollars for expenses, carefully explaining that I was to get receipts whenever possible for whatever money I spent. My handlers were quite reasonable about receipts. They didn't expect me to procure documentation that might jeopardize my assignment. Later, while chatting with one of my handlers, he told me the Soviets were far less flexible. It seems a New York City police officer, undercover of course, had pretended to be a spy for the Soviet Union. Whatever he was directed to purchase by the agents controlling him had to have a receipt attached in order for him to be reimbursed. There were no exceptions. Cheap bastards.

Leaving the room, I made my way back downstairs and wandered around the city for the better part of two hours. As instructed, at 2 P.M., I stood on the assigned corner. Once again, Larry came up to me, "Dick, stay ten feet behind me," and off we went.

The two of us walked into the old police headquarters building on Center Street. I followed Larry to an office. Inside, waiting for me, was the chief clerk of the department. Only an hour or so earlier the man had sworn in a class of several hundred fresh new police officers. Now, one on one, he bade me raise my right hand and administered the oath of office.

From that moment on I was a New York City police officer. Someone in the room handed me my silver shield. I only had a moment to look down at it before someone snatched it away, saying with a laugh, "We don't want you remembering that number." Boy, did I ever want to hold onto that small piece of tin.

Larry then took me outside the office, instructed me to go home, and told me that I'd be called Monday. I left, wondering if the day's events had actually happened or whether it had been some strange dream.

CHAPTER TWO

FIRST CONTACT

The Monday after I had been sworn-in, just as I had been told, the phone rang. "Hi, Dick." It was Larry.

"Hi."

"Well, take it easy. I'll speak to you tomorrow."

That was it. And that was the way it went for a week. I thought I was going to go crazy. I had no idea what to do with all my free time, especially since I had my heart set on doing something, anything, involving police work.

I suppose they got me into this routine of the morning phone call for a number of reasons. First and foremost, it reminded me that although I might be home, I was, in fact, on duty. Second, and perhaps even more important, it would prove to be the normal way I would communicate with my office. Once I settled into the job of intelligence operative, when I had nothing to report I would be required to contact my handler after 10 A.M. Should I have something of significance to report, or anytime I had any information to relay, I would call in earlier.

Clearly, during my first few weeks on the job, when there was nothing for me to tell them, the detectives would contact me when they finished doing their more important tasks.

During one of my initial visits to the BOSSI office, I recall a conversation I had with Lou (Barnie Mulligan). It was when he first discussed my task of infiltrating the Jewish Defense League. His words to me were, "They're like a black cloud on the horizon." I believe that at that time, the department had no real idea as to what level of threat to public safety Rabbi Meir Kahane and his group posed. Up to then, the JDL and its small band had generated a good deal of publicity by staging some annoying demonstrations, causing disruptions of public hearings on school issues and committing a few assaults on members of other extremist groups.

One morning soon after, it was Teddy who called. He instructed me to walk past the Ocean Parkway Jewish Center that evening. A JDL demonstration was to take place there and the detective told me to pick up some JDL leaflets. I was to do nothing more, Teddy was very specific about that. Just walk by, accept a couple of handbills and be on my way. Teddy then said we would meet a day or so later when he'd show me what to do with the literature I picked up as well as how to write the report required of me regarding the contact.

Finally, a mission! A quest! That day seemed to drag on forever until, shortly before 6:30 P.M., I set out for the nearby train station. Although I owned a little VW bug, the directions from Teddy had been clear, "Take public transportation. We'll reimburse you."

Like the good little soldier I was, I took the nearby D train, thereby taking nearly an hour (most of that time spent waiting for the train and walking to Ocean Parkway from the McDonald Avenue train stop) to travel what would have been less than a twenty minute car ride.

During the trip I remember feeling as if I possessed some secret. I wasn't just some guy among the other guys sitting on the subway train, I was an undercover police officer on an assignment.

Some assignment.

Eventually I found myself on Ocean Parkway. This is a main north/south route when traveling from one end of Brooklyn to another, with lights at every intersection. The homes along my path were neat one and two family brick structures, built quite close together, with trimmed lawns out front. Walking down the wide boulevard, up ahead I caught sight of a group of people loitering in front of the Ocean Parkway Jewish Center. Teddy's admonition, to simply stroll by and pick up some literature, was instantly forgotten as I stepped up to the small crowd to listen in on some people arguing.

The gist of the discussion seemed to me to be whether or not the JDLers – most of those involved in the debate were wearing buttons with that organization's name on them – would disrupt the meeting which Mayor John Lindsay, who was then in the middle of his mayoral campaign, would be attending. The consensus of those present was not to cause the JDL any embarrassment. However, it was soon obvious that all within the organization were not of like mind.

It seemed to me that I had stumbled into the middle of a long and ongoing debate involving some recent decisions made by the Board of Education. The issues revolved around the conflict between Jewish teachers already established within the system and new minority hires.

I causally stepped up to one of the men wearing a button. A stocky thirty-year-old, he had no hesitation in discussing the organization with me.

With some pride he told of an incident that had taken place in the Catskill area of upstate New York the previous summer. A poor section of the state, it was, rightly or wrongly, thought of as a place where a significant number of Jewish people from the city enjoyed taking their summer vacations. The fellow said that some local kids had been terrorizing a nearby Jewish bungalow colony. The young men had knocked over garbage cans during the late night hours while at the same time shouting anti-Semitic epithets at the mostly women and children who lived there during week days.

The owner of the colony had called upon the JDL to help the people out. So it was that one night, instead of confronting some frightened women, the five young men faced a group of angry, and armed, JDL members. According to the man I spoke with, the stuffing had been beaten out of those guys. Which seemed to me to be a perfectly reasonable thing to do.

After that, the fellow bragged, there was no more trouble at that bungalow colony.

Leaving with a bunch of leaflets in my hand, I retraced my hour ride on the subway back home. Once settled in, I sat down and typed out a report on the night's events.

The next morning Teddy called. He seemed pleased when I told him how my little task had gone. He informed me that he would show me how to properly word my report, set up an index and cross reference all names, organizations and locations so they could easily be found again. I was directed to clip out a coupon for JDL membership from one of my leaflets, fill it out and, with a personal check for the dues, send it off to JDL headquarters in Manhattan.

Once more I found myself waiting for something to happen. This time it took over three weeks of non-action on the part of the JDL before I was able to convince my BOSSI handlers that I should make an inquiry as to my membership status.

I was still not used to being a police officer, because, except in the most technical sense of the word, I wasn't. Without badge, gun or training I was just a young man hanging out. My desire was to do something important and all I had was lots of time on my hands. To this day, I don't care much for vacations, so I found this down time quite difficult to deal with.

After making the second phone call to the JDL, it became clear that it was fortunate I had gotten permission to contact the organization again. The disorder that reigned at JDL headquarters would have had my membership application lost forever.

Two weeks later I received a call from the Chairman of the Midwood Chapter, Rabbi Shapiro. A soft spoken and gentle man, he told me the date and time of the next meeting to which I was invited to attend.

In the meantime, I had been directed by my police superiors to lay some groundwork to shore up my cover. I enrolled as a student at Brooklyn College and also took a job as a taxi driver with the Terminal Taxi Company in midtown Manhattan. I even joined the union. The department would pay my dues.

God sometimes smiles upon children, drunks and young dopey cops. And every now and again he has a good belly laugh.

The JDL meeting was to take place at 9 P.M. in the basement of a Brooklyn synagogue. Being the inexperienced officer that I was, I showed up wearing a suit. But I was to discover that the other male members who attended that meeting clearly did not subscribe to *GQ*. I found myself surrounded by a mix of mostly young men, the best dressed of whom, except for the neatly attired Rabbi Shapiro, wore the garb of blue collar workers; dungarees, work boots and flannel shirts being the order of the day. As I sat there, nervously fidgeting about, it seemed to me that I most obviously did not fit in with the rest of the group. A few of those at the meeting were middle-aged, most were in their late teens to early thirties. Perhaps a total of twenty or so people were in the room, five of them women.

The Rabbi opened the meeting. Just as with my very first contact with JDL members, here again I found discord. To the members sitting before him, Shapiro spoke of the internal damage done to groups when they bickered among themselves. Once again it became obvious that some of those present had concerns about the militancy of their fellow members. The younger members wanted to get into action, any action, while the more mature members had no desire to cause problems for themselves or others. After his brief talk, the Rabbi attempted to pick up from where the previous meeting had broken off.

Shapiro began by seeking volunteers for various chapter committees. Having been cautioned earlier by my superiors to take it easy and go slow, I refrained from raising my hand. In fact, if anything, I made as if I wasn't there. It didn't help. As the Rabbi scanned the room full of rowdy, unshaven young men and tired, middle-aged working people, he spotted me in my gray suit and I was doomed. I, along with two other men, was assigned to the Security and Defense committee.

By the next meeting I was made that committee's chairman.

My daily ritual of the brief morning telephone call went on for some weeks. Except for the rare demonstration, where other JDL members and I handed out leaflets, there was little for me to report. But my handlers were not at all upset with how things were going. BOSSI was a most professional intelligence gathering organization. Its leaders knew that acceptance of a person into a group cannot be rushed without risking the investigation. And it was made clear to me that such a risk was to be avoided.

From organized crime to the Palestine Liberation Army, if the group had any potential for harming others or causing disruption to society, it might well be targeted by police intelligence. Indeed, some generations before me, during the Second World War, a young undercover police officer had had two merchant marine ships torpedoed out from under him in his capacity as a working crew member. His real job was to infiltrate any Nazi group operating in the New York City dock area. I was told that after he surfaced from his intelligence-gathering role, he eventually rose to the rank of Inspector.

BOSSI was a unit which had many names since its inception around the turn of the century: Bureau of Special Service and Investigation, The Italian Squad, the Radical Bureau, the Bureau of Criminal Alien Investigation, the Neutrality Squad — there were others. The goals of the organization remained constant although the threats continued to change: gather information, stop violent crimes, and protect citizens. Unlike the vast majority of municipal law enforcement agencies whose purview is limited to working within their local areas of jurisdiction and rarely outside of it, New York City police officers assigned to BOSSI traveled around the nation and the world in the performance of their duties. When I eventually surfaced and was assigned to the police academy to attend the recruit school, a number of other newly surfaced BOSSI undercover officers were also in attendance. Being older, and not recruit officers, we tended to hang out together. The group was a potpourri of former members of the Black Panther Party, Young Lords, American Communist Party, Students for a Democratic Society and, of course, the Jewish Defense League.

One of the guys had been under for nearly fifteen years and was a second grade detective. He once told us a story of the time he'd gotten some Communist literature in the mail. Somehow one of his relatives had found out about it and confronted him. All the undercover officer could do was tell the man that that was what he believed in. They hadn't spoken for over ten years. Even now that the detective had surfaced, he laughed and told us he still didn't want to talk to the guy, a relative who he had never really cared for anyway.

As far as my assignment went, it soon became clear to me that the Midwood chapter of the JDL was really no more than a backwater component of the larger organization. Whatever action there was would be at the main headquarters, then located in Manhattan at Fifty-sixth Street and Fifth Avenue. I knew that I had to somehow create a legitimate reason to get myself over there.

Ignoring the cautious approach I had been dictated to take by my handlers, I used my position as the Midwood chapter's Chairman of the Security and Defense Committee to volunteer to go to the main office and pick up some leaflets the little chapter would be distributing.

It was a good move, albeit an aggressive one. My superiors, I am sure, would have much preferred I'd been invited to go to the JDL headquarters rather than volunteer. But I couldn't endure all the waiting around I was doing. I wanted to get into the action; screw this "take it easy" crap.

Upon showing up to the midtown Manhattan office I immediately found myself interacting with a number of key players within the JDL. The reason I gave for being there was both truthful and verifiable. Simply put, I wanted to pick up some pieces of literature for a demonstration some of us from the Midwood chapter were going to conduct in Brooklyn.

Avraham Hershkovitz was the first JDLer I came into contact with. A chubby six foot one, he was a young man with a serious demeanor who wore a yarmulke atop his head. It seemed to me then, and in my future contacts with the man, that he rarely ever smiled or laughed. Later I would learn he had been born in a concentration camp. His father, separated from him and his mother, had been killed at Auschwitz only seven days later. That fact alone seemed sufficient to me to account for his fatalistic view of life.

He took me into a small side storage space and picked out handfuls of JDL material stacked flat on metal racks. I chatted with Hershkovitz as he picked and chose the various items. Seeing the activity around me, leaflets were being shoved into envelopes, phones were being answered, someone was cranking on the handle of a mimeograph machine, I asked if I could I give him a hand while I was here. He said, "Sure," and put me to work.

I was seated at one of the many desks around the office, a large stack of envelopes placed in front of me. My job was to stuff them with whatever circulars were required. In this case, there was to be a demonstration in front of the Soviet Mission to the United Nations in a few weeks and announcements had to get out. As I dutifully folded the pieces of paper, I overheard the office manager, Andrew Melcher, whisper to one of the others sitting nearby to be careful, the telephones were tapped. I asked myself what it was they had to be so careful about but, of course, kept quiet and continued doing my little job.

Glancing about I sensed the place had an air of anarchy about it. Mail seemed to just lie in heaps and the only semblance of order appeared to come from Melcher. He was older than the rest of the young people in the office, perhaps forty, I guessed. A tall thin man with a moustache, he seemed to be trying in vain to keep the whole chaotic mess together.

I caught only a glimpse of Rabbi Meir Kahane that day. He was on the telephone in his office and didn't come out while I was there. He wasn't a large man. He was clean shaven and had dark eyes and black hair, and, as with Hershkovitz, a yarmulke rested on his head. My impression was that he seemed very intense and quite preoccupied.

The rest of those present were busy scurrying about the hectic office. The place was pretty much of a jumble: the furniture was an uncoordinated mix of colors and fabric; metal and plastic chairs, old wooden desks were placed randomly about the room. Half a dozen telephones sat atop mismatched shelves and end tables. The office's style might be best described as eclectic tenement.

Other than myself, there were three young men in the office, all purportedly college students although during my time with the organization, I rarely saw any of them with school books. Besides Hershkovitz, there was Ralph Kaufman and stocky Adam Kauss. Kaufman was a thin man in his early twenties. Swarthy, with a thick black "Fu-Man-Chu" moustache, he had a deep Israeli accent. On that day he hardly spoke to me, and for some time after I only knew him by his alias, Josh Weiss. Kaufman was a very cautious man. In the coming months I would get to know these men well.

Dutifully stuffing my envelopes, I took the opportunity to ask Hershkovitz just what was required to be an active member with the JDL. He seemed to brighten up and said, "The guys in this office are crazy. They'll do anything, they don't care. I was arrested yesterday and if I have to go out and get arrested today, that's okay."

For the next several weeks, I'd show up at the JDL office whenever it seemed prudent, that is, whenever I could find a legitimate excuse to do so. Otherwise, I'd take part in JDL sponsored demonstrations. During this period, the most active arena the organization was involved in was its fight in support of Soviet

Jewish immigration. So it was natural that the place where we demonstrated was the Soviet Mission to the United Nations, a tall building that took up a large chunk of real estate on Madison Avenue and Sixty-seventh Street. A rugged gray iron fence surrounded the outer portion of the structure. The design looked altogether too sturdy to be purely decorative.

There was an ongoing battle for territory opposite the front entrance to the building between JDL members and the New York City police department. Kahane wanted his people to be permitted to picket and chant right up against the building. NYPD brass didn't want them anywhere near the place.

The initial agreement reached with the police was that the department would permit two dozen demonstrators on the side of the street opposite the Mission. The bulk of demonstrators, sometimes numbering in the hundreds, had to be content with chanting and picketing on Third Avenue. From time to time, the twenty or so people opposite the Mission were relieved by people from the larger group.

It didn't take long for me to become recognized as a regular by a number of those who took part in these demonstrations. No one asked me why I was there. After all, they thought the activity worthy of their time, so it was natural for them to assume I was of the same mind.

CHAPTER THREE

THE DETECTIVES

By union contract, once sworn in as a New York City police officer certain benefits automatically accrued to me. Not that I had even given such things much thought (in truth, when I joined the force I had no idea how much my pay was to be), but the fact was that I had to be paid, earn and take vacation time, even follow a certain procedure when sick. On the other hand, the last thing the New York City police department wanted was for me to indicate in any way, by word or deed, that I was a member of the force.

Naturally, in order for my deep undercover assignment to be successful, there could be no Richard Rosenthal listed among the thousands of police officers on the rolls of the department. So simply getting paid posed a problem. The matter was solved easily enough, I was given my money in cash. Undoubtedly some bank was taken into the trust of my handlers, I'm sure only to the extent required for the transaction.

I was directed to come to the office once a week. There I would be paid. Sometimes I'd be debriefed, and I'd complete my reports and whatever other paperwork was required of me. The detectives, most being senior experienced men, were careful not to comport themselves around me (and I assume the other operatives) as they would normal police officers. No police jargon was used in front of me. It was made clear that I was never even to go near a police station, lest some member of the JDL spot me and conclude I was a police officer.

In retrospect the hands-off approach to my training in law-enforcement might have gone a bit too far. Except for the aforementioned instructions on how to write up my reports and do other associated and rather basic ministerial tasks, I received no training from my handlers. No tradecraft, no spy v. spy instruction. I believe the theory was that to be a successful undercover officer, one had *not to be* a police officer. Ergo, knowledge of the job and its customs was viewed as being both counterproductive and potentially dangerous.

Perhaps. But a few hints on how to perform in the field might have proven helpful. For example, one Sunday morning, some months into the investigation, I received a phone call from Kaufman, one of the more important JDL members. It was an urgent invitation to come to the JDL office and in fact was to be my indoctrination into the most active cell within the organization. Immediately upon hanging up with the man, I called the detective on duty that weekend so as to let him know where I was going. Had the JDL member had any sense, he would have phoned me back a minute or two after our conversion. After all, who would I be calling early on a Sunday morning, right after speaking with him? Any call I made to my police contact should have been done from a public telephone.

It was indeed fortunate for me that JDL members were as naive in their attempts at being terrorists as I was in my efforts to uncover their criminal activities.

The office where I met the other members of the department was a small, nondescript place in the middle of Manhattan. The building must have been around awhile, as the elevator leading up to our offices, on the second floor, as I recall, was ancient, with scissor-type sliding metal grates. The department had rented the location anonymously. The men assigned there (all detectives) wore conservative business suits and carried no visible firearms. I don't remember the name of the bogus company stenciled on our door. The landlord, so Bill informed me, had no idea what was going on inside.

The office consisted of several fairly small rooms. Once I entered — I was instructed to come neither early nor late, otherwise I'd risk bumping into one of the other undercover officers — I would be ushered into a room by one of the BOSSI detectives. Inside was a manual typewriter along with my files. I'd spend an hour or so doing my paperwork, which, as the investigation continued and became more complex, fell more and more behind.

From the moment I began my career in police intelligence, the message given to me by my superiors and handlers was consistent: take your time. The greatest concern the BOSSI detectives had was that I might be rushing things. After all, they had had operatives in the field for as long as twenty years — a number of them retiring from the force never having held their shields, worn a uniform or carried a gun. BOSSI and its previous iterations had been around since the turn of the century. The officers working in it knew that there was no way an undercover police officer could force his or her way into a target organization, especially so if that organization was involved in activities which merited penetration.

It was a difficult lesson to accept for a young cop who, as Harry Tice, one of the detectives who worked with me on the investigation, liked to say, was "full of piss and vinegar."

It was also made quite clear to me that while I might observe, I could not act. At least, not take part in any serious criminal actions. BOSSI's goal was for me to be the proverbial "fly on the wall." See and hear everything, take part in as little as possible. And, I was most vigorously instructed, under no circumstances was I to initiate some illegal activity. Entrapment of innocents, or even the appearance of entrapment, was not my job. Bill once complained to me that during the trial of one of their cases, a bombing attempt thwarted by a BOSSI operative, the defense counsel argued that no such bombing was in fact going to take place. The attorney told the jury that his clients wished only to scare someone, and that if the New York City police department hadn't interfered with his clients by arresting them, the innocence of their intentions would have been demonstrated by their ultimate actions. Bill couldn't understand how police officers could have permitted individuals about to plant explosives to do such a thing. He was exasperated, exclaiming, "What do they want us to do?" Bill confused the words of the plaintiff's advocate with the desires of society and the goals of a police force.

I found it interesting that there were never any comments made about the JDL's philosophy or ideology. The detectives around me appeared to be completely indifferent to such things, analogous to surgeons whose job it was to extract a diseased organ but who had no particular interest in the identity or personality of the patient. They were, however, very interested in my estimates as to the number of demonstrators who might be attending any given gathering. As my penetration into the JDL increased, my superiors would continuously ask me for my best guess as to how many people I thought would show up to specific future demonstrations. It was explained to me that generating a sound assessment of the numbers of citizens who might participate in such activities was done in order to assign an appropriate number of police officers to a given public meeting. It was one of our primary functions. After all, manpower was expensive. A single large demonstration could generate tens of thousands of dollars in police overtime costs. If possible, it was the goal of the department to assign the correct number of officers to each given event.

As close as I worked with the men and women assigned to BOSSI, it was rare for any of them to be out in the field with me. In many ways it was a lonely assignment. When the fiction writer and former intelligence agent John LeCarré used the phrase "out in the cold" in reference to an operative, I knew what he meant.

Only my parents, my mother's parents in Brooklyn and, of course, my wife, knew of my work. Who we are assumed to be in society is largely a function of what we do to earn a living. To most of the world, including all my relatives and friends, I wasn't doing very much of anything. My dream, to be a member of the New York City police department, had indeed come true. But nobody could know of it.

My working alone in the field likely posed a challenge, albeit a different one, for my BOSSI bosses as well. At the time I didn't think much about the problem the detectives would have in their supervision of me. After all, what would have stopped me from making up some bland but false reports about a routine demonstration should I wish to just stay home. While such a thought never even crossed my mind, the fact was BOSSI had one other police officer, Richard Eisner, assigned to infiltrate the organization. Of course I wasn't told of Richard's existence, and he was kept unaware of mine. We even dutifully reported on the conversations we had with one another. Had our reports not substantially coincided in detail it would have been a dead giveaway that something wasn't right.

CHAPTER FOUR

BECOMING MORE INVOLVED

Within a few months of my showing up at various JDL sponsored demonstrations, as well as performing the assorted odd task at its headquarters, opportunities began to arise which helped me win the confidence of those around me.

One day, while hanging around the Fifty-sixth Street office, a call came in from a cemetery on Staten Island. At that time, a city-wide grave diggers' strike was taking place. This posed a serious emotional, as well as practical problem, for Orthodox Jews. People who practice this set of beliefs do not sanction the embalming of their dead. Generally, this results in no health problem, as their rites require that their deceased loved ones are to be buried within a strict, and quite narrow, frame of time, usually twenty-four hours. But with the ongoing grave diggers' strike, bodies from every religious group began to stack up. Fortunately for those concerned it was a cold January.

One family, their father's remains resting in a plain wooden coffin as is the Orthodox Jewish custom, had attempted to dig the grave themselves. When some of the unionized workers stopped them, the family called on the JDL for help.

So it was that Kaufman, a number of other members, and I headed out to the island. Kaufman, driving a rented car, flew through the streets of New York City like a mad cab driver on a holy mission. He treated stoplights as if they were yield signs and streaked around vehicles on the right if there was an available inch to squeeze by. As scary as the ride was, it did make for good travel time. We made it from midtown, through Brooklyn and across the Verrazano Bridge over to Staten Island, and on to the cemetery well within an hour. By the main gate, were a number of police officers standing in front of men in work clothes who were carrying picket signs. Opposite them were several members of the deceased man's family, holding shovels and pick axes.

Kaufman wasted no time. He hopped from the car and joined in on the ongoing, and heated discussion. It was clear to me that the police were there simply to keep the peace and weren't about to give permission for one side or the other to do anything. In his thick Israeli accent Kaufman tried to reason with the union members. They were adamant. Graves were dug by union grave diggers. No one else was allowed to dig a grave. So, as union grave diggers were out on strike, no graves were going to be dug.

Kaufman didn't argue. He simply nodded and walked away from the fray. Quietly he motioned for the son of the deceased, as well as the small group of JDL members, to step away from the larger group. He whispered, "This is the way it is. Police permission or no, we're gonna dig this grave. So, grab the tools and let's go. Either we're gonna dig or we're gonna get arrested trying."

Everyone shrugged as if going to jail was the most natural thing in the world and each of us went over to grab a tool. As we picked them up, the son gave each of the JDL members the name of various members of his family. "You're Bernie Brown. You are Harry Greenblatt. Your name will be ..." That way it would only be family involved in the matter and he hoped the police would let it go.

We all returned to the place where the police officers stood watching the union workers milling around. The son calmly announced to all within earshot what was going to happen. He hardly got a word out when the debate began again, this time even more acrimonious than before. It started to become very loud when another police car drove up. Inside sat a florid-complexioned, white-haired police sergeant on whose nameplate was an unmistakably Irish name, something like Murphy. As he eased himself out of the cruiser, the dead man's son went over to him. In a quiet restrained tone he explained what was about to happen. He then said to the sergeant, "I just want to bury my father." As soon as his words came out, the union members made it clear that no such thing was going to take place.

The sergeant looked around, took a deep breath, eyed the picketing workers, and softly said, "This man is going to bury his father."

The officer's tone of voice left room for no further discussion. The little band of JDL members did what we had come to do.

For a while after that incident, besides my attending a number of demonstrations and getting myself better known among the JDL members, little took place which I considered to be significant enough to generate meaningful police intelligence. I would show up at the various demonstration sites: Madison Square Garden, the Soviet Mission to the United Nations, sometimes the United Nations itself. I'd fall in with the other protesters, walk in a circle and chant whatever it was everyone else was chanting in support of Soviet Jewry. It was, in fact, the one part of the job that I truly disliked. I'm not a shy person, but to hold up a sign while marching around the street in the middle of a freezing Manhattan winter, yelling slogans with a bunch of zealots, wasn't my idea of police work and, furthermore, was simply something which I was not comfortable doing. Beside which, the people passing us on the street seemed to stare at us, probably wondering if we were nuts. I could have told them, "Yes, we were."

One of the activities which I did enjoy during this period was my weekly Sunday evening trip to the Palmach (Hebrew for defense) Gun Club. Club members utilized an old military range located in an armory on Bedford Avenue, in northern Brooklyn. Eventually I became one of their instructors.

It was a massive stone building, built around the turn of the century. Although dungeon-like in their dreariness, these old armory ranges were designed to withstand the battering of military rifle practice. How people could have fired such powerful weapons indoors — they must have certainly suffered serious hearing loss — is beyond me.

Most of the time the members of the club would shoot either .22 rifles or take turns borrowing one or another of the various members handguns, mostly .38s. I enjoy shooting, and anyway the NYPD was paying for my ammunition (a bona fide expense no less!).

In New York City, I have found that a number of citizens who enjoy owning and shooting firearms — the legitimate ones, at any rate — seem somewhat conflicted over their dealings with the police, the department, and their hobby. Permits for handguns were then, and still are, quite difficult to obtain in the city. So, as with narcotics, guns, handguns in particular, took on a value and meaning far beyond the reality of what they actually were, machines designed to expel lead pellets at high velocity.

People believe the strangest things about firearms: a shotgun blast will cause an automobile to burst into flames and blow up, a bullet fired from a handgun will physically knock a person down, a single round from a pistol will stop a determined assailant. Nonsense. But after watching such feats performed a mind numbing number of times on television and in the cinema, and not having any practical experience otherwise, what else would people think?

In fact, shotgun pellets, even the larger ones used by police such as double-O buckshot, when fired into an automobile, simply puts holes into a car's sheet metal. There is no reason a fire, and certainly never an explosion, would result. As far as what is depicted on movie screens as the result of gunfights — whether they be fantasy westerns or James Bond shoot 'em up scenes — the script writers have altered the laws of physics to suite their needs. Clint

Eastwood's facing down half a dozen villains on a dusty western street and instantly immobilizing them with his deadly accurate rapid fire, this from models of handguns that were historically known to be slow to get into action, marginally reliable at best, inherently inaccurate and only of limited power, defies logic. A gunfight, in truth, was then, and is today, often the prelude to hand to hand combat.

A century ago a "cowboy's" handgun was more often then not whatever weapon a person had the money to buy at the moment. These men could ill afford the expensive cartridges needed to practice often enough to become truly competent marksmen. Many of the handguns they carried were small caliber revolvers. They did indeed shoot one another, not in face-to-face "slapping leather" or "quick draw" contests, but more often at arm's-length distance over some petty dispute at a poker game and after much consumption of alcohol. Their handguns were lethal less at the moment of discharge than a few weeks later, due to the blood poisoning that resulted from the filthy little slugs festering in their victims' bodies.

A .38 special revolver fires a lead pellet that weighs about a third of an ounce. The bullet is spit out of the weapon's muzzle at a speed ranging from 800 to 1,000 feet per second. That's just under the speed of sound. Upon entering the human body, a modern well designed projectile will begin to expand, damaging and sometimes destroying whatever tissue it pushes through and past. Unless a human is struck in the central nervous system, or there is a violent disruption to the body's ability to pump oxygen rich blood to the brain, the battle has just begun. That is why animals are slaughtered by a bullet to the brain and the muzzle of a professional killer's pistol is placed on the back of the victim's head.

When a person is fighting for their life, adrenaline rushes through the body. In an actual gunfight, frequently there is no pain associated with the initial wounds. That comes later, which is why it sometimes takes dozens of handgun rounds to stop a determined adversary. When the police are involved, and a civilian is struck numerous times, the cry "excessive force" rings out. The fact is, it may take several minutes from the time a lethal wound is inflicted, to the moment the body stops functioning. All the while, the threat that person presents is very real.

A retired Marine Corps major once told me of an incident he witnessed in Vietnam. His platoon was ambushed in an open area. The marines charged the enemy. The marine running next to the major, firing his battle rifle, took a round which blew his head off his body. The corpse continued running forward, discharging his weapon until empty, then collapsed.

There is neither glamour nor glory involved in a gunfight. In the real world there is never a soundtrack playing. There is no script to follow. A gunfight is a bloody, chaotic, frightening mess which often ends up in a tie; the result being two or more dead or wounded people. Survivors of gunshot wounds are often permanently crippled. Life is not a movie.

One thing I've long noted is the strained relationship between many of the firearms retailers within the city and police officers. As it is the responsibility of the police department to license and oversee these establishments, firearms retailers are under the closest scrutiny from the police. Over the years I've noticed a kind of "love-hate" relationship which builds up on the part of the legitimate gun sellers in their attitude toward the police. These people identify with the police because, like officers, they have access to firearms. Furthermore, they tend to be of a "law and order" mindset. Yet, I have observed on a number of occasions an animosity toward police officers hidden just below the surface. Perhaps these feelings come from jealousy; by New York State law the police need no permits to carry firearms and they can freely purchase whatever weapons they wish.

In addition, firearms retailers generally know a fair amount about firearms minutia, prices, weapon model numbers and their histories, but very often possess little skill nor knowledge about the practical application of weapon craft. Theirs is a limited knowledge, born of familiarity with their wares but found lacking in the need to use them in the day-to-day way law officers must. Police officers, particularly those working in busy precincts, must be ready to use their skills with hand weapons whenever they are on patrol.

I recall one incident, this was well after having surfaced from my undercover assignment, when I walked into a gun store in Manhattan. The establishment was run by a husband and wife. Perfectly pleasant people. I noticed that the woman was carrying an eight round capacity .25 caliber pistol on her hip, a truly abysmal handgun caliber for self-defense purposes. It suffers the unfavorable characteristics of being just powerful enough to be considered lethal, and thus a deadly weapon in the eyes of the law, yet is so under-powered a round as to be truly ineffective in its ability to stop an assailant.

When his wife left the store's front room, I asked the gentleman why she was armed with such a handgun. He replied, "For the firepower." The poor fellow didn't have a clue.

By state statute, in New York City it is the police commissioner who is the firearms licensing authority. The average citizen will find it virtually impossible to obtain an unlimited carry permit, although with sufficient perseverance, a citizen can secure a permit to own and transport his or her handgun, unloaded and in a locked case, to and from legitimate firing ranges. In any case, a handgun permit of any sort will take the better part of a year to obtain and in the process will cost nearly two hundred dollars in fees. Furthermore, the department does not make the task an easy one.

So I suppose that it should come as no surprise that I have observed a good deal of resentment against police officers on the part of those who would like to be able to carry a concealed handgun but who are unable to come up with a sufficiently good reason for the department's licensing unit to issue them one. The same frustration applies to many other individuals who, after having spent much time and aggravation seeking a full carry license, only manage to eventually secure for themselves a limited permit.

One fact I soon learned, and dutifully reported, was that many of the Palmach's shooters had secured limited handgun carry permits, for target shooting purposes only, yet were toting their handguns around wherever they went. During that time there wasn't the strict requirement that the transporting of handguns to and from ranges had to be done only in locked containers. So it was that when I was at the Palmach range, there was much discussion among those present about how best to take advantage of what was at the time a loophole in the law.

One of the men who I met, carried a folded, paper bull's-eye target in his jacket pocket. It was yellow and brittle with age. He believed that should he be stopped and searched by a police officer — an unlikely enough event to occur to this mild looking, neatly dressed gentleman who always wore a small crocheted skull cap pinned to his thinning hair with a bobby pin — this target would supply him with the plausible explanation that he was just headed to a shooting range.

Right.

Long bull sessions took place in which the participants debated how one should comport oneself when, as a pistol license holder, one was confronted by a challenging police officer. One fellow advocated standing on one's "constitutional rights," while others recommended a softer approach.

Herbert Grebler, a man in his early forties who I knew from the Midwood Chapter of the organization, where he served as co-chairman, regaled us with the advice he had received from the owner of a large and well known gun store in Manhattan. Grebler told us the store owner advised one of his customers that should some police officer observe that the man was armed (an individual who in fact possessed a full carry permit), and should that officer ask to see the man's pistol permit, the man should show his permit but refuse to hand the document over to the officer. A nitwit recommendation if ever there was one.

To refuse a lawful order to hand over a pistol carry license, so an officer could check its validity, would at minimum result in a confrontation with the officer and likely lead to the revocation of the permit.

But it mostly seemed to me that what I was hearing at the Palmach Gun Club were the gripes of legitimate, honest citizens, concerned for their personal safety and wishing to protect themselves, who were at the same time feeling very guilty for the deceit they had to take part in in order to do so.

CHAPTER FIVE

WORKING MY WAY IN

At every meeting, every time I showed up at a demonstration or at JDL head-quarters, I always felt self-conscious because of who I really was and what my actual purpose was among these people. I never felt as if I was like any of the others in the room which, upon reflection, seems odd to me. After all, my background had to be similar. My family had lived in Brooklyn for a number of generations. I attended public schools there. My parents weren't particularly observant Jews but we held a Passover Seder and I attended Hebrew school, albeit not being that institution's most promising student.

It wasn't too long into the investigation when I came to sense that at least some of the other JDL members believed I was not who I pretended to be. Herbert Grebler, fellow member of the Midwood Chapter and the Palmach Gun Club, certainly had his doubts.

Although he and I had spoken at the various demonstrations we'd attended together, it was while we took turns driving each other to and from the Palmach range on Sunday evenings that I struck up an acquaintance with the gentleman. Grebler was about my father's age. He wasn't an intimidating man; he was beginning to lose his hair and spoke with a kind of nasal intonation. An educator by profession, he was bright and inquisitive. It didn't take him long to recognize that something was amiss with my background as I had explained it to him.

In truth I did attend Brooklyn College as well as drive a taxicab part-time. But Grebler wasn't buying it. Unlike the other members of the JDL, young and crazy guys who themselves rarely gave a straight answer as to who they were or what they were about, Grebler was an honest, mature and law abiding man. Furthermore, as a person who had worked professionally with hundreds of young people over the years, and with us spending as much time together as we had, he was able to evaluate me with far more detachment than the others.

Grebler, probably at first unsure as to whether I was simply making poor life decisions or was indeed someone other than I claimed, asked me if I'd like to take a battery of aptitude tests in order to help give me some direction as well as meaningful goals. It was a very nice, and I believe, a genuine offer, except that in my capacity as an undercover police officer all I really wanted was to get as much distance from the man as possible.

His concerns became clear to me during one conversation we had. We were at one of the Midwood chapter meetings when, after everyone had left, Grebler took me aside. He told me that he felt that various law enforcement agencies had planted individuals within the JDL. He then went on to tell me that he thought that was okay, that they were simply performing their legitimate function.

There was no reason for him to say these things to me unless he had serious reservations as to who I was and what I was doing there.

This was trouble and I wasn't sure how to deal with it. After all, everything I had told the man was true; it just wasn't the whole truth. All I could do was continue with my facade and hope for the best.

In the JDL, as with any organization, one had to "pay one's dues" before being accepted as part of the group.

I had been told by my police supervisors that it would not be a bad thing for me to be arrested during one of the myriad demonstrations I was attending. At the same time, they made it clear to me that there were definite limitations as to what I could and could not do in the line of duty. To remain within the confines of the law I could watch and listen but not suggest, lead, or make policy. Above all, I was not to commit any serious crime.

Undercovers, by the very nature of their work, can easily find themselves in extremely difficult situations. Bill Gorman related one such incident to me involving a deep cover officer.

The man had infiltrated the Black Panthers. Another member of that group decided he wanted to kill a police officer. Taking the undercover into his confidence, he informed the officer that he wanted to do it that very night. The pair drove out on to the FDR Drive, a major New York City highway that runs along Manhattan's East River. The other man's plan was to fire his weapons from the Manhattan side of the East River, directly across at those officers coming out of the Four-Four Precinct in the Bronx and conveniently visible from his proposed vantage point.

The undercover had little choice but to let the impromptu plot play out as long as he dared, hoping something or someone might intervene and abort the plan at the last minute. Such was not to be. When the other man prepared to open fire there were no further options open to the officer. The undercover pulled out his pistol and placed the aspiring cop-killer under arrest, thereby ending his undercover assignment and with it tossing aside the years of work it had taken him to get where he was within the organization.

As Bill told the story I asked myself what I would have done under those circumstances?

At about this time there was a great deal of talk at JDL headquarters about the situation between France and Israel. The French government, under pressure from several of the Arab states, had recently reneged on a deal to sell a number of gunboats to Israel. It was thus determined by the organization's leaders that the JDL would cause as much embarrassment to the French as possible and that the French President, George Pompidou, would receive some negative attention. The matter was made much simpler by the fact of his upcoming visit to the United States.

The actual nature of the relationship between France and Israel at the time was open to conjecture. This was especially apparent to me when I was told by one of the younger JDL members that someone from the New York City office of the Israeli Consulate, upon hearing of the JDL's plans, contacted Kahane. The Israeli official specifically asked that members of the organization "behave" when the French president came to visit.

Diplomacy is a subtle art and international relations sometimes take many subtle turns. In fact, the vessels in question, ordered years before what was then the most recent Israeli/Arab war, were eventually "stolen" by the Israelis and successfully brought over to Israel. That theft, of course, saved the French from the embarrassment of selling the gunboats to the enemy of the Arab countries, who, at the time, were major purchasers of French military goods.

It seemed, however, that the JDL was going to "help" Israel even when such support was neither sought nor desired.

Early on the Sunday morning of the demonstration, Meir Kahane, the political and spiritual leader of the organization along with several dozen of the JDL faithful, myself included, milled around the street in front of the headquarters building, waiting for the cars and buses which would take us to Washington, D.C.

I lucked out. Instead of being stuck in a crowded and noisy bus for the long trip I managed to hitch a ride with some of the guys in Melcher's station wagon. Melcher stayed behind.

En route to the nation's capital I engaged one of the JDLers in what was to me just another juvenile bull-session. There was a great deal of bragging about what his particular sub-unit in the organization was going to do; they'd be taught to handle firearms, make bombs, learn karate, and so forth. Then the discussion moved on to the young man's relationship with some purported motorcycle gang, their three wheeled Harley-Davidson motorcycle with its mount for a .50 caliber machine gun, talk about live grenades, and on and on. Finally, the conversation culminated in his asking if I were capable of slitting a man's throat, or blowing someplace up. And, by the way, could I get him plans to construct a firearms silencer?

Once we got to D.C. we joined the hundred or so JDLers standing around and were all directed by some senior JDL members over to the National Press Club. There I saw Kahane in an intense discussion with a police officer, who was making it clear to the Rabbi that no demonstration would be allowed within five hundred feet of any building in which Pompidou was appearing.

Kahane left the officer and walked over to our group. He told us to walk, single file, in front of the Press Club entrance. By the looks on the faces of the several dozen officers lining the street I could see they were not amused by this tactic. What I tried to keep in mind was the suggestion given to me by Bill Gorman a day or so earlier. He told me that I should try and get myself locked up during whatever demonstration took place, so as to solidify my position within the JDL. Here I was, a guy who had never even gotten a traffic ticket, about to do something that would have me arrested. Swell.

Telling myself that I was obeying both the wishes of the New York City Police Department as well as those of the head of the JDL, I dutifully joined in with the rest of the snaking line of JDLers moving toward the front of the Press Club's entrance way. No sooner had one of the younger members in the group come up to the front gate when he raised his fist and yelled, "*Am Ysrael Chi!*" (Israel lives).

The Washington, D.C. police needed no further invitation. Men in blue moved in and began to arrest the unresisting demonstrators. Now, my problem was that I needed to get busted but the officers kept going around me. I'm a reasonably big guy, five eleven and over two hundred pounds, so officers were grabbing everyone around me, demonstrators who also happened to be smaller than me. Finally, I had to literally put myself in the path of one of the officers, almost having to insist on being taken into custody.

Once he realized I was not going to be a problem, he relaxed. We both smiled and I was taken over to the police van.

So, there I was, handcuffed, sitting in the back of a Washington, D.C. police paddy wagon, being taken off to the local lock-up. Sitting in the back of the wagon, among the other JDL members I'd been arrested with, I had to remind myself that this was a good thing. I was doing what everyone wanted me to do, the detectives at BOSSI as well as the people running the JDL. Nonetheless, as it was the first time in my life I had ever been taken into police custody, I had very mixed emotions about the experience. And there was one other dilemma that I faced. Undercovers rarely have any back-up officers present and that day was no exception. As far as I knew, no one from the NYPD was in Washington that day. Ergo, at that moment none of my handlers from BOSSI were aware that I was headed off to jail!

After a short bumpy ride on the wagon's hard bench the rear door was unlocked and the dozen or so demonstrators in the truck's rear were ushered into a booking area. Everything around us was gray, concrete, and depressing. We were placed three or four to a cell and each of us in turn had our photos and processing information taken.

I had never been in a police lock-up before. Although the officers handled everyone in a professional manner, the feeling of confinement was not a comfortable one. Adding to the anxiety level was the fact that there was no way to know when we'd be getting out. For hours I sat among the other JDL miscreants on the hard cell benches. We were all tired, hungry and bored.

Guys chatted quietly amongst themselves, a few tried to sleep. But it was my luck to be in the same cell as Grebler. Now he really had me. He asked me, "How come your wife never comes to any of these demonstrations?" Before I had a chance to formulate a response he shot back with, "And how come, every time I call your house, either you answer the phone or it just rings?"

Here was where I had a real problem. My wife, a German citizen and only in the country a few years, had a very distinctive accent. She didn't like to answer the telephone if she could help it. Although her grasp of English was superior to many native-born Americans, she found that speaking on the telephone in a foreign tongue (English, for her) was the most difficult part of communication. I can attest to that. While in Germany, I had little trouble dealing with people face to face in their own language, but telephone conversations were another matter entirely. Gone were all the subtle communication clues, facial expressions and hand gestures that we give to each other when we speak in person.

And anyway, the last thing I wanted the JDL members to know was that I was married to a non-Jewish German.

Finally Grebler confronted me, albeit quietly: "You're driving a cab half-assed and you're a half-assed college student. It just doesn't add up. I think you're a federal, state or local agent infiltrating the JDL. I mean, who would know? You say you're from out of state. Sure, you're impossible to verify one way or the other. It's all too pat. And you never seem pressed for money. It doesn't add up."

After his little soliloquy he added that he hadn't mentioned his concerns to anyone else in the JDL. I didn't believe him for a minute. Grebler's view of my situation was perceptive and correct. I found it hard to argue with him on the issue or defend myself. I mumbled some lame reasons for what I was doing with my life and how I chose to live it and let the matter rest.

After several hours we were all released from the holding cells. None of us ever went before a judge. My assumption at the time was that by then the French president must have moved on to some other part of town where we wouldn't be able to bother him. The rest of the day was a bust. As was common with the JDL organization, many ambitious plans had been made but little follow-through done to ensure their successful implementation. So for several hours we just hung around the Capital's streets, waiting for directions until it was time to leave.

By late afternoon, when it became apparent that somehow the number of people heading back to New York City numbered more than the vehicles still remaining in D.C., Kahane, another member, and I went out and rented a U-Haul pick-up truck. It took us till 2 A.M. to get back to JDL headquarters.

After the accusatory conversation I had with Grebler, I reported my dilemma to Bill Gorman the next day when I called into the office. Bill didn't seem overly concerned about the matter (but then, he wasn't out working in the field as an undercover either). He told me to just continue doing what I was doing. I was not convinced this whole thing would work itself out that easily and whenever I was at demonstrations at the Soviet Mission or elsewhere, when I spotted Grebler I'd attempt to keep my distance.

A few days later, the French president was in New York City. More demonstrations were held. It was after one such demonstration at the United Nations, while hanging out at the JDL headquarters on Fifth Avenue, I was called into the Rabbi's office.

The reason the JDL had such tremendous impact, and generated such concern both for our government as well as the Soviet Union's during this time, was deceptively simple. The head of the organization, Rabbi Meir Kahane, knew well how to manipulate the press, public sentiment, and the governmental structure. In furtherance of his aims, he had a small group of devoted followers, most quite young, who would do whatever the man told them to do, without hesitation or consideration for their own welfare. In truth, without Kahane there was no JDL. He was the organization.

Most of those within the group with whom I came into contact were reasonably responsible middle and lower middle class people who had various grievances and concerns they wished voiced. It seemed to me then that they represented a segment of the Jewish population — simple and hard working people — whose needs, fears and concerns were not being addressed by the larger and more established Jewish organizations. The JDL more closely responded to the anxieties of these people and their disquietude over crime, neighborhood racial frictions, job security, as well as the perceived peril faced by Soviet Jews, than did any other Jewish organization of the time.

The long-standing, conservative, and far more proper Jewish groups seemed nervous and somewhat frightened by the JDL, and especially with the aggressive tactics used by its members. For a hundred years these organizations had taken great pains to blend in with the larger American community. The high profile taken by the JDL seemed to threaten them with the potential loss of their hard won positions in society. Furthermore, I believe they did not wish to instigate reprisals (economic, social, and perhaps even physical) for what they viewed as the JDL's loud championing of unpopular positions (for example, Kahane's support of the Vietnam war), from those of the surrounding majority.

Nor were these fears without historical foundation. In Europe, from where most of the forebears of American Jews had come, they had found that when holding little real power in a society, a minority depended to a great extent on the sufferance of those around them for their security, livelihood and even their personal safety. The grandparents of those assimilated American Jews didn't leave Germany or Eastern Europe primarily in order to find a better life in this country. They left because they didn't wish to be killed.

So for generations the tactic of not drawing undue, especially controversial, attention to itself had become the American Jewish establishment's way of life. Perhaps it might be crudely thought of as the Jewish equivalent to Uncle Tom-ism. This non-aggressive position was challenged by the JDL. When ads appeared in New York newspapers showing a group of young men wearing yarmulkes and brandishing metal pipes, chains and martial arts weapons, over captions which read, "What's a nice Jewish boy doing here?" establishment Jews became very uncomfortable indeed. The slogan, "For every Jew a .22," did nothing to allay their concerns.

The entrenched Jewish establishment fought back, mostly by denouncing the JDL, trying to assure non-Jewish Americans that this little band was but a tiny assembly of crazy, sociopathic people, an anomaly among the larger group, wholly unrepresentative of the majority of American Jews. On occasion the major organizations even engaged in a smear campaign against its leader, Rabbi Meir Kahane.

But Kahane was, in the first instance, too smart for them and, even worse from the establishment's viewpoint, indifferent to their opinions of him. He didn't care what "respectable" Jews felt, believing, with some substance, that the act of simply being a respectable Jew was no protection in the face of serious threats to the group. He once used the analogy that some Jews — this particular dissertation was about those who sought peace with the Arabs in Israel — were like lemmings, small suicidal rodents that from time to time threw themselves into the sea. In Kahane's view, Jews who were more concerned about form than substance, who felt guilty about doing what was in their own best interest (in this case keeping as much of the Arab territory as possible), were like lemmings. And he went on to state that he did not wish to be viewed as a small rodent.

He knew that passive behavior in the face of vicious anti-Semitism hadn't helped the large assimilated German population of Jews in the thirties and forties, and he believed, wrongly but with deep conviction, that our imminent loss of the war in Vietnam would bring a similar backlash against the anti-war groups who helped to cause this defeat to happen. Kahane felt that Jews who had been involved within the anti-war movement had been too vocal and visible among those in the front ranks. The loss of this conflict, he opined, would be such a traumatic and disheartening event that it would bring terrible retribution down on the heads of American Jews from the larger conservative society.

He knew that in our nation, with its valued traditions of free speech, and, especially in historically liberal New York City, as long as a certain line was not crossed, a group of dedicated and bold people could create major disturbances with little cause for concern about legal retribution. Kahane was thereby able to generate much publicity for the issues he espoused. Shouting down a political candidate, chanting in front of a political or social event, picketing at a foreign mission and handing out leaflets were actions which were, for all practical purposes, virtually and absolutely protected by the United States Constitution. While tipping over of bottles of ammonia and other little tricks used to disrupt visiting Russian performances were not lawful, Kahane was nonetheless confident that such actions were reasonably safe activities to engage in within New York City. After all, the government of the Soviet Union did not elect mayors (or district attorneys) in this city. Nor were there many Americans who felt either love or kinship for that particular foreign power.

But, Kahane's fears and goals eventually took him beyond such relatively harmless acts. He was certain that the American Jew was about to face the same kind of holocaust threat as their European counterparts had only a few decades earlier. Kahane believed in the teachings of Zev Jabotinsky, a Polish Zionist of the 1920s and '30s. Jabotinsky had seen the danger coming. He had warned his countrymen of their peril, but he had been ignored. Kahane was determined not to go unheard this time around. To Kahane it didn't matter whether the Jew was orthodox or non-observant, living in the Bronx or Kiev. Danger to one was danger to all. The fact that he and his followers could get their hands on Soviet property and persons in New York City and cause discord and trouble for the Soviet government, for a nation where Jews were being persecuted and denied unlimited immigration to Israel, just made his task a bit easier.

That the actions of the JDL had become a terrible political problem for the city of New York, the State Department, and the United States government in general was of no concern to the Rabbi. That the JDL was proving to be an insufferable embarrassment to the comfortably entrenched Jewish hierarchy, only meant to Kahane that those other Jewish groups simply were unable to see the future repression headed their way.

My nature is not to be a passive individual. Therefore I found it no surprise that a number of Kahane's beliefs seemed to me to be prudent and reasonable. For example, I believe in the right and the duty of individuals to stand ready to defend themselves, their families, and their property. Personally, speaking from the experience of having thirty years' law enforcement service behind me, I have no fear of an armed population. Indeed, I find it hard to imagine how a free citizenry could exist without reasonable and ready access to firearms. I am comfortable in stating that after my long years within the law enforcement community, I do not possess an innate distrust of either our government or those who serve it. On the other hand, I am aware how quickly such seemingly benign situations can change. History is most clear on this matter.

Today's growth of neo-Nazi and other violently racist and anti-Semitic, anti-government groups notwithstanding, the fact is, Kahane turned out to be wrong in his interpretation of what the future would bring for the American Jewish population. But I have no doubt that, had he kept to more reasonable acts in the pursuit of his goals, there is no way of knowing how far he could have gone politically or as a Jewish spokesman.

The man was neither a saint nor a sinner. His enemies have attempted to portray him as some demonic dangerous zealot, sort of a Jewish Nazi. His supporters depict him as the reincarnation of the militant Zionist leader, Zev Jabotinsky. I don't know which viewpoint is correct. What I do understand is that he was a complex individual who passionately clung to his beliefs.

Ironically, Kahane was conservative in his views relating to law and order. I think he genuinely liked police officers and wanted them to be free to do their job. I recall that after one of the many demonstrations the JDL was involved in, and in this case after some minor confrontation with the police, Kahane mentioned an incident he had been involved in years earlier. He told those around him of the time when, as a teenager, he had demonstrated by the New York City docks where a British warship had come in. This was before the state of Israel existed and during the period when the British ruled Palestine. Kahane told us that the police broke up the demonstration by freely hitting those taking part with their nightsticks. He then commented, "Now those were cops!"

I found the man to be brave, almost to the point of being reckless. When facing conflict he would not take the expedient road, but rather would stay true to his beliefs, even if that meant inconvenience or danger. He once told me of an incident that occurred on a Friday afternoon when his plane landed later then expected at Kennedy Airport. Observant Jews are not permitted to drive on the Sabbath, which starts at sundown on Friday. Although he lived twenty miles away, instead of violating his religious principles, Kahane walked home. I also watched him lie with abandon when dealing with the media and saw him manipulate, control and mesmerize men and women with his charisma.

Kahane has been called a racist. Yet, during all the times I had been with him, I never heard him utter an ethnic slur of any sort. This was true even during the conflict which arose when Black activists sought to take control of the city's school system, clashing with the large numbers of Jewish teachers already in the organization. My sense then was that Kahane was not anti-Black. Indeed, I felt at the time that he was sympathetic to the plight of African-Americans. What he was, however, was most forcefully pro-Jew. Yet, a few years later, I had an opportunity to observe him on television being interviewed in Israel by that country's news media. As he trembled with rage, Kahane demanded, spit out really, the words that the "Arab dogs" should be thrown out of the country. The only thing about the man I am absolutely sure of is the fact that he loved the Jewish people and he loved Israel. There was never any doubt in my mind that he would have gladly given up his life for their cause. Perhaps, that is what ultimately happened. At the age of fifty-eight, he was assassinated in New York City, while lecturing on the necessity of American Jews to emigrate to Israel.

I was taller than Kahane by several inches. As I entered his office and stood before the man, he began by saying that a number of people in the organization had spoken highly of me and I had been recommended for a leadership position within the JDL. But as he went on, I could tell exactly where his words had come from. "You seem too good to be true. You spend a lot of hours with the organization and your background is in many areas which are of interest to us." This was verbatim Herbert Grebler.

He then referred to my military intelligence training, Russian language capability and my knowledge of firearms. I silently reflected on just how well BOSSI had chosen me for this particular assignment. Kahane went on, asking me questions about where I had come from and what I had done in the military. I answered truthfully; the truth being, ironically, the one, really the only, protection I had. I simply omitted the fact that I was also a New York City police officer.

After several minutes of this gentle interrogation, I noted that he wasn't looking directly into my eyes, that he stuttered ever so slightly, a sign to me that he was uncomfortable with the role he was playing. He then asked, "How would you like a position as a JDL chapter chairman?" Aware that my police superiors would never permit me to take on such a leadership role, I stammered out some excuse about why that would not be practical. He went on, telling me that he needed some stability in the JDL Youth Group. "We have a lot of young people in the organization but they need direction." Eventually he let that thought trail off. Almost as an afterthought, perhaps even with a tone of apology, he told me that the JDL had to concern itself with infiltrators from various organizations.

Once more I dodged what seemed to me a well directed 'bullet.' My answers as to why I was doing what I was doing within the JDL seemed to me extraordinarily lame. Viewing myself as how I believed an outsider would see me, I felt that I stuck out in a most conspicuous manner when I was around all these people. My ability to speak in complete sentences, the way I dressed, my high regard for responsibility and distrust of braggadocio, even my everyday socialization was just too different. Yet this very intelligent man didn't see through me. I can only attribute this to the fact that there were other members who marched to the beat of a different drummer, as well as the fact that he was busy to the point of distraction with all the demands he faced in running his organization. He seemed to have very little help. Nor, I suspected, any experience in dealing with the myriad personalities (some quite damaged) which surrounded him. Melcher, the only stable, mature adult in the office, beside Kahane, seemed to me to be an able office manager. Yet, he was consistently undermined by the young men who spent most of their time at JDL headquarters. They would rarely follow directions as to how he wanted things run in the office: simple things, such as how to answer the telephone, where to file the ever-mounting paperwork, how they might comport themselves in order to permit the most basic organizational structure to function around them. It was the same young people who Kahane had told me needed stability, who would obey only Kahane himself; the same wild young men who were both the greatest strength and most significant weakness of the organization. By harnessing their youthful absence of fear, their selfless dedication and readiness to do violence, Kahane realized he had the power and ability to impact the greater society far more than by sponsoring mere demonstrations. Paradoxically, with them around, he was aware there would never cease to be chaos within the JDL. These young men, and some women, upon whom he so depended were, by and large, troubled and often dysfunctional people. Why else would they risk being arrested, winding up with a police record, even going to jail for the JDL. The organization gave them a purpose and purpose was what I observed most of them needed in life.

I rarely ever met the parents of the young people within the JDL, most especially the parents of those who were the most involved. It certainly seemed to me that for a number of these youngsters the closest thing they had to family was the organization.

At any rate, Kahane chose to permit youthful anarchy to take precedence over whatever structure Melcher might have offered. In fact, only a few months after this conversation with the Rabbi, Melcher, the one predictable person whom I observed in the office, severed his affiliation with the JDL.

Kahane asked me if I could participate in a demonstration at the New York Cultural Center a few days hence. They'd be exhibiting Soviet photos and I was to be in charge of a group of demonstrators. Sensing that this was some kind of small test, I took it on. It turned out to be no big deal. Although later in the day, other JDLers would throw paint on the various exhibits, my little group and I just did some picketing and had a minor confrontation with a security guard inside the building. But our action was sufficient. When we got back, I stepped into the Rabbi's untidy office. After listening to the details of what had transpired, Kahane nodded, and let me know he was satisfied with how things had gone.

I was about four months into my assignment when another opportunity came along which would help me establish my credibility within the organization. It seemed that Melcher's son, Kenneth, was having trouble with a number of kids at his high school. As luck would have it, I happened to be at the JDL office when a few of the members were going to take care of the matter.

Kaufman, a few other young men and I got into Melcher's station wagon. We headed out to Long Island where the Melcher family lived.

Our weapons were meager. I saw three of the guys carrying so-called "nun-chucks," a martial arts striking device popular (through Kung-Fu movies) with a number of the more aggressive JDL members. They were nothing more than two sticks (they could also be metal pipes) connected at one end by rope or chain. The motion of the stick held in the hand increased the force of the end striking your enemy. At least, that was the theory. We also had a few small aerosol cans containing some kind of pepper spray chemical. It was the most "armament" I'd seen these guys carrying to date.

On the drive out to Long Island I sat alongside Kaufman. At one point he turned to me and asked if I was carrying a weapon. I told the man that I had nothing on me, at which point he reached into his shirt pocket and pulled out a razor tool. Holding it up for effect he inquired if I had any qualms about 'cutting' someone? It didn't require any deep thought on my part to respond with a definite yes to that question. Kaufman shrugged and put the razor away.

The question that haunts the undercover is always, Did I say the right thing? I figured I had. It certainly would have been hard to sound truthful had I come back with any other answer. While I might be playing a role, the fact was, I was still me.

Once we got to the high school things began to get strange. The young Melcher was sent out to try and locate his tormentors. Now, it had never been made clear to me what the problem was between him and his schoolmates. Nothing was ever said to indicate that the problem, whatever it was, had any relationship to the JDL or its goals. So, I suppose, what we were doing was, we were going to 'out-tough' some tough guys.

At any rate, young Melcher stepped up to a group of eight of his fellow students who were standing around the schoolyard and began speaking to them. I didn't notice any unusual behavior or threatening body language from the small group when, all of a sudden, Kaufman opened the car door and ordered, "Let's go!" We tumbled out of the car. At that point some of the teenagers started to make fun of the JDLers. Kaufman went over and began what might be best described as a James Cagney routine.

"Look, you fuck around with Molotov cocktails…" First I'd heard of this, but I remained silent. "Well, we use dynamite. You fuck around with Kenneth and we are gonna fuck around with you. And you're gonna be dead."

In his heavy accent, it sounded like a good speech to me. It must have been, for a short time later the vice-principal of the school came outside to find out what was going on. To that gentleman, Kaufman gave a little speech, telling him that if the school couldn't stop the harassment of Kenneth Melcher, Kaufman could.

Having done our bit to intimidate those at the high school we moved on to find another of the young man's harassers. A few miles away we stopped in front of an auto repair place. Kaufman and Kenneth got out and walked behind the building. A few minutes later the two came tearing around from the back of the garage, yelling, "Shotgun!"

It appeared to me that at the moment that Mr. Kaufman's charms had failed him. Just as we were to take off, two Nassau County police cars showed up. The officers brought the two groups together and a general amnesty was declared.

We then all left for the Melcher home. According to Kenneth, the house was going to be firebombed. So Kaufman decided that we would set up an all-night guard.

We pulled up to a pleasant looking but modest suburban home. Inside, once things got settled down, out came the hardware. There was a .22 rifle, an old .32 caliber handgun of dubious lineage, and a far more formidable riot shotgun. This last weapon had a twenty-inch barrel with a magazine that went all the way to the muzzle, making for a capacity of eight 12-gauge rounds. Since the thing was loaded with Magnum 00 buckshot, that is, twelve pellets in each cartridge, a person with a fully loaded shotgun could put 108 lead slugs in the direction of anyone they wished.

The senior Melcher and Kaufman discussed their tactical alternatives. The consensus reached by the two was that anyone who set foot on the property carrying a Molotov cocktail would be shot immediately.

During the course of the evening JDL members kept coming to the house. By late evening, twenty of JDL's finest, virtually all kids, were hanging around the house, waiting for the bad guys to show up. I wondered where their parents thought they were. Kaufman had even gotten hold of a second shotgun for the occasion.

Now, the one riot shotgun had certainly sparked my interest. It was a legal weapon to possess, although its only practical purpose was for use against people. With the appearance of the second shotgun, identical in make and model to the first, I wondered how many more of these were in the hands of the JDL. As casually as I could manage, I asked one of the young men manning the barricades what the story was with those guns. He, a camper at the JDL's summer camp in Ellenville, New York the previous season, shrugged and said, "I don't know, they've got plenty."

"No kidding. How many?"

"Well, I've seen around ten of them, anyway."

The household suffered no attack during the evening hours. So it was decided to go out and locate Kenneth Melcher's harassers. Kaufman, three other JDLers, and myself jumped into the Melcher station wagon and went out looking for Kenneth's tormentors at various teen hangouts. Fortunately for all concerned, we found no one to beat up and returned to the house.

So, here we were, huddled together, armed with at least three harmful, two certainly most formidable, weapons, waiting for God knows who to show up and firebomb the place. No one really seemed to have a good handle on what we were about, what was to be accomplished, or how the matter would finally be resolved.

One short conversation I had with Kaufman did make it all worthwhile. It was after midnight. As he and I stood shoulder to shoulder, peering out the ground floor window at the quiet suburban street, he asked, "How come you don't get more involved with the JDL?"

To an undercover police officer, such a question, when asked by one of that officer's primary targets, is like manna from heaven. Keeping my enthusiasm in check, I calmly replied, "Well, you know, it's tough, working and going to school. But I'll try and get down to the office more often."

We all left at four-thirty in the morning. No attacks had occurred, and to the best of my knowledge no one ever burned down the Melcher house.

CHAPTER SIX

OY!

One Sunday evening, while I was out of the house, Herbert Grebler called. Frauke, who had answered the phone, told me he would be coming over shortly to pick me up so we could go to the Palmach range.

My heart sank. Here was the most suspicious of the JDL members, a man who had no confidence in my cover story, and who now had just become aware that I was married to a German woman. I figured, that did it.

When he arrived, I left my ground floor apartment and, before he could make his way into the house, jumped into his car. I still hadn't figured out what I was going to say. However, before I said very much, I noted his attitude had changed. As we drove along, he let me know that he now understood why my wife didn't like to answer the telephone. In effect, he began to confess to me. He explained that his wife, too, was foreign-born. She was Latin. With great enthusiasm he began to extol the virtues of marrying a non-American woman. It was clear from the tone of the conversation, although I didn't ask him, that his wife, like mine, was not Jewish.

Just the fact that we shared this little secret seemed to make all the difference in the world to the man. For the moment he was completely oblivious to the flaws in my cover story. As far as Herbert Grebler was concerned, I was cleared of suspicion.

A week later I got another call from Grebler. He was pushing for me to go with him to what he described as a major JDL activity on Sunday, May 10th. He went on to tell me that our job would be to sell buttons at the Israeli Day parade. I was not thrilled. It seemed to me that selling buttons was no way for me to get anywhere in this investigation. I put him off with a noncommittal answer.

My initial doubts about being accepted into the group, at least by a majority of the members, had proven largely unfounded. The variety of personalities attracted to the JDL proved sufficiently diverse so as to disguise any anomalies

I might have presented to those around me. Of course, that didn't stop me from getting cocky and making the occasional major blunder.

Religious Jews (and Moslems) are forbidden to eat certain kinds of food, or even to mix specific food types within a group. For example, it is absolutely not allowed for an orthodox Jewish person to eat shellfish, fish without scales (say, shark or swordfish), or pork products. Nor is it permissible for a person who holds such beliefs to eat meat and dairy products at the same time. A person who follows these customs and laws is referred to as keeping Kosher.

Now, I knew all about such beliefs. Although neither my parents nor my grandparents observed these rituals, my great-grandparents most certainly did. Therefore there was no excuse for what I did at the JDL office one day.

I guess I was feeling pretty comfortable with the situation by that time. So, I let my guard down. As a bunch of us sat around various tables stuffing envelopes or performing some similar monotonous activity, it was decided that lunch was in order. We were going to have some hamburger place deliver the food. When it was my turn to speak up, without any thought I said, "A cheeseburger and a container of milk."

All of a sudden the whole office was on my case. People were yelling at me, asking me what the hell was I doing? I didn't even realize for a moment, a long moment, what I had said to create such a fuss. Then it hit me. Most of those around me were, if not Kosher, at least sensitive to the feelings of those among us who were. They'd never insult those people the way I just had.

The colloquial Yiddish phrase that might be used to describe someone who commits such a dopey indiscretion is *putz* — a word roughly translated as 'penis,' but taken to mean anyone who acts with ridiculous stupidity.

I dutifully mentioned my gaffe in that day's report. Of course, the problem any law enforcement agency has is that when they have to select someone to infiltrate a possibly dangerous militant organization, it is unlikely that their candidate is the kind of person who would ever join such a group. Not many New York City police officers probably aspired to be members of the Black Panther Party, Students for a Democratic Society, or the American Nazi Party. The JDL membership was by far made up mostly of reasonable and benign Jewish citizens. But their identification with their religion was certainly stronger than my own. On the other hand, not all that many observant Jews wind up walking a beat in New York City.

The next time I came in for my weekly meeting with BOSSI detectives they were waiting for me. As I hadn't made a big deal out of the incident in my report, it should have occurred to me they had gotten the information from another source. But at the time, I wasn't in a thinking mood. A female

Jewish detective who was on the BOSSI staff was in the office waiting for me. In her hand she held the book, *Guide to Being a Jewish Housewife*. She led me off to one of the side rooms for added training. The ignominy of it all.

I have long forgotten the name of the detective assigned to instruct me (to be a Jewish housewife perhaps?) on basic Jewish etiquette and customs. I don't know what they expected me to learn from her. How does one teach another not to do stupid things? At any rate, I was not amused by her attempted lesson in Jewish ritual. I, perhaps a bit brusquely, assured her that I understood the error of my ways and that I would try to be more sensitive in regard to such customs in the future. Oy!

Around this time in the assignment, things began to happen more quickly, cheeseburgers or no. One Sunday morning a bunch of us were at the newest JDL headquarters office, a large loft-like room on West Forty-second Street between Ninth and Tenth Avenue. I noticed that most of the 'heavy hitters' were there: Rabbi Kahane, of course, plus Ralph Kaufman, Stuie Cohen and his girlfriend Eileen Garfinkle, Avraham Hershkovitz and his new wife Nancy, Michael Fisher, the organization's head karate instructor, along with a couple of dozen others. One of those present was Richie Eisner, my fellow New York City police officer also assigned to BOSSI. Of course, neither Richie nor I knew the other was a police officer.

Kahane began by explaining to those present that the JDL was growing very quickly. The organization would soon purchase (or be given) a five-story building in Manhattan, in which the JDL would build, among other things, a firearms range open twenty-four hours a day, seven days a week. He then went on to explain how the organization was going to try out a new structure system. They'd keep the regular chapters as they now existed but would introduce a separate infrastructure, whereupon groups of no more than ten members, specifically, young members, would meet. They'd come together every two weeks and would receive special training — in exactly what, he refused to be more specific. They would also be taught how to fight.

What Kahane was saying, in effect, was that he would be breaking down the active membership of the organization into cells. I knew that I had to be chosen.

Kahane went on to talk about the day's activities. The JDL had kept up the pressure on the Soviet Mission to the United Nations. It was the only way Kahane knew of to torment the Soviets in the hopes that that government would permit more open immigration of their Jewish population to the free world. This Sunday would be no exception. Kahane would lead fifteen volunteers to the front of the Mission gate. This was a direct violation of the agreement with the police that, up to then, had kept demonstrators across the street and in controllable numbers. He told the assembled JDLers that they would hold a *Seder*, a religious service involving the blessing of significant ritual foods, right there in the middle of the sidewalk.

As photography was a hobby of mine, from time to time it permitted me the luxury of being present at some of the JDL's activities without directly partaking in them. My job that day, specifically assigned to me by Kahane, was to take photos of the event. No need to scream, or pass out buttons, shove leaflets in people's faces or avoid getting arrested. He couldn't have given a police officer a better job.

So it was that around 1 P.M. Kahane led a small group of strollers nonchalantly down Third Avenue and turned into the Mission's block on Sixty-seventh Street. The police who stand guard by the front gate thought nothing amiss as these normally dressed people, some carrying a table, others with small packages in their arms, sauntered down the street in their direction.

Once Kahane was in front of the Mission, he stopped, opened the brown paper bag he was carrying and chained himself to the iron gate. Someone else, appearing as if from nowhere, attempted to set up the table and hand out prayer books. In less time than it takes to recount the story, an officer appeared with a bolt cutter, snipped the shackles binding the few JDL members who had been able to get themselves chained to the fence, handcuffed the lot of them and marched them all to the Nineteenth Precinct, a mere fifty yards away.

As this was going on, the other members of the organization cheered and chanted. In any event I don't think the first group managed to stay in front of the Mission for more than a couple of minutes. Melcher told me to call the *New York Daily News* and offer them my exposed film. I eventually brought the film over to the newspaper but, alas, they did not see the same value in the photos that I did, and they chose not to publish them. Eventually, I handed them over to the BOSSI detectives.

A few weeks after Grebler had called to ask me to come to the May 10th Israeli Day parade, another member rang me up with the same request. This time, I decided not to waffle and agreed to be there.

By early May, I had become a regular at the various JDL functions and around headquarters. Over the previous few months I had let the members become aware of my background in military intelligence and my knowledge of firearms.

One evening, shortly after showing up at JDL headquarters, I was invited to a seminar by Kahane. We left the office, got into the Rabbi's compact car and headed over to the east side of Manhattan. The conversation in the car was a wide ranging one. He confided to me that the building they had been offered, the one in which he had hoped a firearms range might be built, probably wasn't going to work out. The structure had so many code violations, it wouldn't make economic sense to fix it up. Kahane was nevertheless adamant about the JDL setting up some sort of firearms training facility. He told me that he knew the head of the Palmach Gun Club and mentioned the name of one of the instructors. I let the Rabbi know that I too was an instructor in the club.

His interest level immediately rose. Always intense, his thoughts raced on as he asked me questions about the types of firearms most suited to training his organization's members. The discussion turned to the summer camp. It was his wish for the campers to move into what he referred to as 'big bore' weapons. He specifically mentioned the .30 caliber M1 carbine (a weapon which, in fact, fired a round not much more powerful than a handgun cartridge).

He went on, "My goal is to have a hard-core group of fifty tough individuals. People trained in how to handle firearms."

At that moment Kahane didn't say to what purpose he wanted to put these people. But I was already aware of his belief that there would be a vicious backlash against Jews from the larger American community once we were defeated in Vietnam. Above all, he was most anxious for his people to be able to defend themselves, against any threat.

As we spoke it became clear that Kahane had little knowledge of weaponry. When he spoke of .30 caliber carbines, the lowest powered military long arm ever adopted by the United States military, as 'big bore' weapons, I didn't correct him. If that was what he considered a powerful firearm, so be it. In hindsight, I suspect it was this very need on his part for individuals such as myself, people who possessed expertise in arcane areas, which compelled an otherwise astute man not to look more deeply into those around him. Pulling up to our destination he said, "My main problem is getting money to buy things." The emphasis placed on the word 'things' clearly indicated to me that he meant weapons. He honestly believed that American Jews would soon be facing a German-style holocaust.

Once we got back to the main office I saw that the place was fairly crowded. In one of the rooms, a number of youngsters, their fathers by their sides, were being interviewed for the upcoming JDL summer camp. Stepping away from the hubbub of strangers, I hung out with some of the guys I'd gotten to know: Lenny Brown, Kevin Bendel, Ron Hershman and Jake Wiesel.

The seminar was to have begun at 8:30. But at a quarter to the hour the phone rang. For some reason, the Rabbi picked it up. I noticed that at once Kahane became absorbed in deep conversation with the other party. When he hung up, he looked over to where we were standing and called the group into his office. He instructed us to get over to Brooklyn right away. We were to drive to Public School 167, on Eastern Parkway and Schenectady Avenue, a racially troubled neighborhood. The ethnic mix in that area was of several groups, but for the JDL's purposes it was only important that there was a large Hasidic community in conflict with their Black neighbors. This particular situation which we were going to be involved in would take place at a community meeting where a number of the local Jewish residents felt they needed the clout of the JDL's 'finest.' So Kahane assigned the six of us to go to the meeting to do what we had to do to protect our people.

Kevin Bendel, Jake Wiesel, Morty, Ron Hershman, some fellow I didn't know and I went downstairs and got into a car. We were all pretty big guys. Bendel, Wiesel and I went over two hundred pounds each and the other guy wasn't much smaller. Still, as we headed toward Brooklyn, I couldn't help wondering just what we were getting ourselves into. On the way, Hershman had us stop by his apartment building in lower Manhattan. He jumped from the car and was soon back with a small can of tear gas and a blank firing pistol. I silently hoped that if he did have to pull the damn piece, the other guy wouldn't respond with the real thing. The others carried weapons as well. Wiesel had a metal pipe. Morty and the other young man carried nun-chucks. As for me, all I was armed with was my good looks. BOSSI, for very logical reasons, didn't want their untrained, un-credentialed people running around the city armed. Anonymity was our only protection. Yet, there were times during this investigation that I found this was not enough.

By the time we got to Eastern Parkway and Schenectady Avenue where the school was located, no one was around. A man on the street informed us that the meeting had been moved to an empty room over an A&P three blocks away. We decided to park our car and walk.

Although I was born in Brooklyn, I wasn't familiar with this area. It had occurred to me as I drove along Eastern Parkway, which once must have been a wide and handsome European-style boulevard, that the homes now looked tired and the area had fallen on hard times. I recalled that, when I was younger, the neighborhood was considered an orthodox Jewish enclave. Yet now, all the faces I saw on both sides of the streets, as well as on the Parkway itself, were Black. I also knew that the neighborhood's transition from the one ethnic and racial group to the other had not been an easy one. And what we were heading into at the moment was just one small conflict among the hundreds, if not thousands, which preceded it.

The A&P was a small supermarket. A door alongside its main entrance led to a narrow stairway to the second floor. Once inside we found ourselves in a modest sized room packed with people. I figured there had to be nearly eighty individuals crammed into the space. Beside the JDLers, there were five other Whites. The rest of the audience was Black.

With no room to maneuver, the six of us put our backs to a wall and kept an eye on how things were going. I don't remember what the meeting was about, only that tempers were mounting and if the situation had blown up we would have been badly outnumbered. I do recall that reasoned debate was not what took place that evening. Different people, White and Black, attempted to speak. From the deliberate injection of chaos into the meeting — there was much catcalling and shouting from the audience — I'm certain that a large number of the people in that room had no intention of permitting anything constructive to come out of that gathering.

A tall man in a leather jacket, sitting next to me, called out, "Let the brother speak!" But as soon as the speaker began, the man added softly, "If he is a brother." I took this to mean that if the speaker voiced an opinion contrary to his own, he had automatically proven himself to be the other side.

The meeting fell apart about a half hour after we arrived. For me, it was a glimpse into the realities of New York City neighborhood racial politics that I had never seen, even though I had grown up only a few miles away.

For all the rancor we encountered that night, I figured the JDLers had been lucky there had been no violence. We would not always be so fortunate.

CHAPTER SEVEN

BREAKTHROUGH

On May 7 Grebler called. He sounded excited, having just been to a lecture out in Queens given by Kahane. He explained that the Rabbi had told the assembled group that two units were being formed within the organization: Oz A and Oz B. My mind immediately went back to the short talk Kahane gave just before we had departed for Washington D.C., about forming the organization into ten-person cells. Explaining that Oz was the Hebrew word for courage, these were to be two very active components of the JDL. The Oz B group would be made up of older members, who would be assigned the less strenuous tasks.

Grebler went on to explain how he had gone up to Kahane and volunteered a number of members he knew for the Oz B group, myself among them. I found it interesting that my former accuser had turned into my new mentor. The man was looking out for me, but it was only the Oz A unit which I had interest in.

The Israeli Day Parade took place the next Sunday, May 10, and the JDL wanted its presence known. I showed up at the Fifth Avenue headquarters building around 9 A.M. The place was quite crowded. Although I knew about a dozen of the people inside there were an additional twenty or so who were new to me.

Orders and assignments were being handed out by Hershkovitz. Two older members were given a bunch of light blue JDL buttons which bore the inscription "Never Again" over a clenched fist imposed on a Star of David. Below that symbol were the words, "Jewish Defense League." I was handed a sheaf of leaflets and the three of us were sent over to Fifth Avenue at the southernmost tip of Central Park, a position which put us along the route of the parade.

With my fellow JDL members I stood around, loudly hawking buttons and giving out sheets of paper to passersby, feeling like a jerk. Here I was, months into my assignment, and all I had to show for it was my standing on a street corner asking for donations. Some job for a gung-ho police officer.

Feeling foolish and somewhat sorry for myself, I wanted to get off the street in the worst way. Such an opportunity arose around 1 P.M. Two young women assigned the same task as my little group stepped up and handed me a bag containing $107 dollars, along with some of their leftover buttons — an act which was sufficient enough excuse for me to return to the office.

By then the place had become much less crowded and I wound up in conversation with a neatly dressed man I hadn't met before, Dave Sommer. A teacher in the New York City school system, he introduced himself to me as the director of the JDL summer camp. He was a bit shorter then me, with a neatly trimmed goatee and mustache. Like most of the other men in the group, he wore a skullcap.

To say the man was loquacious would be an understatement. God, he could talk. Here was someone who neither knew me nor knew who I was, yet he began by telling me he had a number of unregistered .45 caliber pistols, stolen U.S. property, which would be the JDL's as soon as the organization paid for them. He went on about being a member of the Palmach and how he was getting himself a pistol permit. Sommer told me about two long guns he owned, then went into detail about the firearms the JDL possessed. He claimed the group had twenty-five riot shotguns, one of which he had in his house, the rest being scattered around in different locations. In addition, there were three bolt action .30 caliber rifles, including one which had a telescopic sight. All this was news to me and, not long after we spoke, to the New York City police department.

Sommer then talked about the summer camp. Some months earlier I had seen photos of the campers in the magazine section of a New York City newspaper. The photographer took pictures of the boys practicing karate. The article indicated that there were around three hundred campers attending the facility. Sommer smiled and said, "We lie a lot." He excitedly explained that the visiting news people had been told that the campers they were observing were those who were not "out on maneuvers." In fact, the camp's entire complement of fifty youngsters had been standing right before them.

"What about all the other things I saw in the newspaper article," I asked. I ticked off what I remembered: that they had extensive training with firearms, were trained in guerilla warfare, in self-defense, and so on.

Sommer smiled again, saying, "It was easy. I'd just never deny any speculation a reporter offered up. Instead, I'd look around, maybe let my eyes fall to the ground, you know, acting somewhat embarrassed, and tell whoever was asking that I'd rather not talk about it. They ate it up."

Sommer let me know that he hoped to have a hundred campers there this next summer. I let it drop that I was a Palmach firearms instructor, at which point he blurted out, "How'd you like to be the camp's rifle instructor?"

It was as if he had asked me if I'd like to win the lottery. But even as a dopey young cop, I knew this was going way too fast for my own good.

"Dave, wait a second. I got to earn a living. I just can't pack up for a summer and move upstate."

"Hey, don't worry about it. All you'd have to do is come up on Monday mornings. Give them some training for the next couple of days and head home Tuesday evening."

Trying to control my excitement at this stroke of luck, I told him, "Let me think about it. I'd have to work some stuff out. How about if I figure out if it's possible to do and get back to you in a few of days?"

We shook hands and Sommer wandered off to a side office to interview a prospective camper. As he disappeared with a young man and his father behind a closing office door, I wondered to myself if any of the youngsters who applied for a slot at camp ever got rejected?

A couple of days later I wound up driving my cab around Manhattan. This part of the job sucked. My mom's dad, after getting out of the army at the end of World War I, bought a hack medallion for five bucks and spent the next forty-odd years driving a taxi for a living. He worked long hours for little pay, raised three daughters, and I can never recall the man complaining. Me, I'd been given my hack license by BOSSI. It was the real thing, the only problem being that once I was out in the cab and on the street, most of the time I didn't know where the hell I was going. It was boring, riding around the traffic clogged city streets. I found the work to be an unpleasant and mind-numbing waste of time.

I tried not to work this job more than I had to. Although, on occasion I did find it was a good idea to drop in at the JDL office while in my taxi. It certainly helped make my cover more believable.

So it was that one afternoon I stopped by the headquarters. Among those inside were Cohen, Fisher, and Kahane.

The Rabbi called me into his office. He seemed more distracted than usual, even agitated, asking me right out if I would take charge of the yet-to-be-built JDL range. Kahane told me that he'd prefer the place to be legal, with all the proper permits and authorizations, although that wasn't strictly necessary. He was adamant about setting up the facility soon, so much so that he grabbed hold of a *New York Times* lying on his desk and opened it up to the Buildings for Rent section. As he thumbed through the pages, looking for a store with a basement, he told me he wanted all those JDL members who had a talent for rifle shooting to be able to practice as often as they wished.

The whole situation had caught me by surprise and put me off somewhat. The man began to go on about other subjects: procuring weapons, ammunition, targets. I didn't see where all this was heading and had trouble following his train of thought. After all, I had just casually stopped by the office and now I'd become involved in complex planning over firearms ranges and a discussion about the ancillary equipment required for such a project. Caught totally by surprise, I had no idea of the ramifications of what I was doing.

Kahane told me he had many things he wanted to talk to me about. I replied that I had to get my cab back at four-thirty, which was in fact true. I figured I could afford to be a bit indifferent now that my expertise in weaponry had been recognized as valuable to the organization. Furthermore, even with the limited experience I had in dealing with these people, I sensed it wasn't a good idea to show too much enthusiasm when talking about such subjects. I soon left the office and made my way back over to the cab terminal.

On the instructions of my detective handlers at BOSSI, I waited a full week before calling Dave Sommer back. My call was a short one, just letting him know that after thinking it over, I might be able to find the time to give him a hand at the summer camp as their firearms instructor. The conversation ended with us agreeing to meet soon at JDL headquarters, so we could put together a program for the campers.

The next week I received a call from Hershkovitz, telling me to get over to headquarters immediately. He didn't say why. When I arrived at the Forty-fourth Street location — the organization had fully moved over to the Shori DoJo, a martial arts studio — there were around forty JDLers already there. The buzz among those milling around was that we were going to take part in a major action against the Soviet government.

We were eventually given a short briefing by Hershkovitz. He informed us that what we would soon be doing would be illegal and would likely result in our arrests. He asked all of us to be back early the next day, with sleeping bags, extra clothing and food.

When I got home, I contacted Bill Gorman and let him know something big was going to take place. Bill instructed me to go with the flow.

It was a barely seven-thirty the next morning when I showed up at the DoJo. There were already over three-dozen people there, the same faces from the evening before. For over an hour, I wandered around the office, talking to various JDL members in the restless group, listening to them wonder aloud about what exactly was going to happen. Finally, Kahane called us together. Standing on a raised platform that overlooked the workout floor, he matter-of-factly announced that the JDL was going to take over the Park East Synagogue. That particular house of worship had the unfortunate luck to sit opposite the Soviet Mission to the United Nations. Our goal, Kahane continued, was to hold out in the building for several days, trying to remain there until sundown on Friday, the start of Sabbath. While we were there, we would stand on the synagogue's terrace, which faced directly toward the Mission, and broadcast the JDL's thoughts about the treatment of Jews in the Soviet Union. As the Rabbi was speaking, I noted that one of the college-age JDL members, Warren Jansky, was staring at me. I ignored him and focussed on Kahane, who made a point of telling the assembled group there was to be no violence whatsoever within the synagogue.

After the Rabbi's speech, Jansky came right to the point, asking if I thought there was an informer in the group? By now I had had four months' experience being someone I was not. His thinly veiled accusation didn't bother me. I knew he had asked that question to see my reaction. I casually answered that I doubted it and walked away.

The mass of people involved in the synagogue takeover had been told to get over to the corner of Sixty-eighth Street and Third Avenue by subway and bus. Loaded down with cardboard boxes filled with food, knapsacks on our backs, and bedrolls under our arms, we looked like a ragtag army of refugees. It was 10 A.M. by the time everyone arrived at the assembly point. Now a unit once more, we tramped the block over to the synagogue, entered the quiet dark building and, with no one to stop us, occupied the second and third floors. Our stuff went onto the long pews lining the large high-ceilinged rooms.

Almost immediately the structure was sealed off by a wall of police officers who stationed themselves between the Mission and the synagogue. From our vantage point, it was clear that we had taken the police completely by surprise. Well, perhaps not completely. After my call to Bill, he undoubtedly had called on our boss, Lieutenant Mulligan. There were certainly three or four members of the department who had known this action was going to take place. But clearly, my safety and the success of my mission took precedence over any benefit the local command might have garnered by being told beforehand about the disruption that was going to occur.

A large sound amplification system was set up on the balcony overlooking Sixty-seventh Street, which couldn't have been more than twenty-five yards from the Mission's windows. Then someone plugged in the microphone and speakers. Kahane immediately began a diatribe, a very loud diatribe, aimed at the Mission's occupants and audible to anyone within a three-block radius of the place.

After one tirade he called me over and told me to write a speech, in Russian, to be directed at the Mission. As Kahane knew, I had learned the language at a school while in the military and was reasonably competent to do the task. But, as the request caught me by surprise, I suspect the grammar and syntax I utilized in the final product could have used a bit more work.

Nonetheless, Kahane was pleased when I took the microphone and blared out whatever it was I said to the hapless Russians. I'm not sure whether the people inside the Mission were more angry with whatever it was I had attempted to say or to the violence I had done to their beautiful language.

Our takeover lasted several hours. Speaker after speaker railed against the Soviet's treatment of their Jewish population, never letting up. Kahane, when not on the balcony, spoke to those of his followers who were inside the building, lecturing us on the history of Jews in Russia.

Our little engagement was not to go on as long as planned. The police inspector in charge of the precinct, David Fallek, called Kahane to the street to talk to him. He told Kahane that unless the JDL left, officers would come in and arrest the entire group. The two men got into a shouting match more appropriate to bickering fourth graders.

Kahane shouted at Fallek, "You're a Jew, you shouldn't be doing this!"

Fallek became enraged. He screamed back, "Come on Rabbi, we'll fight man to man, just you and me!"

"Hey, Fallek, you've lost your cool." As Kahane walked back into the building he added, "We have nothing to talk about."

At that moment, the police didn't have the authority to enter the synagogue (it was private property) unless invited, or I'm sure Fallek and Kahane would have soon been rolling on the ground.

It took a late afternoon meeting of the synagogue's executive board to decide the fate of the demonstration. The JDL would leave; one way or the other.

Sometime around four-thirty I fell asleep. At a little after 6 P.M. someone shook me awake. I was told that Kahane had called all of us to a meeting. As we sat in the stepped seating of the synagogue, me rubbing the sleep from my eyes, he stood before us and explained the situation.

"We have three options. We can leave as ordered, stay and get arrested, or compromise and leave later, at about seven-thirty."

There was a short discussion among those present. Kaufman made it clear that he was ready to fight. He wanted us to make Molotov cocktails and throw them at any raiding police. It was a mindless suggestion and would have likely resulted in serious fire damage to the synagogue, probable injury to many as well as the major prosecution of those inside. The majority prevailed, with compromise being the final decision.

First we cleaned up the synagogue. Food wrappers, items of discarded clothing, and whatever debris lay around, we picked up. At the appointed time, our little rag tag army filed out of the building. Standing downstairs by the exit door was Fallek. It quickly became apparent to me that neither he, nor a few of the JDL members, had yet to move out of the adolescent stage of their lives. As Michael Fisher, the organization's top karate teacher, stepped onto the street, he called to the inspector, "Hey, Fallek, you want to fight me?"

"Anytime!"

"Right now?" Fisher replied.

"Right here!"

As each approached the other for their mano-a-mano duel, two JDLers grabbed hold of Fisher and two police captains fastened onto the inspector's arms, saving face all around. It was a scene worthy of any elementary school yard.

We straggled back to the DoJo for a debriefing and a seminar conducted by Kahane. Once again he explained how the American Jew had been considered a patsy, a turn-the-other-cheek kind of individual. That would have to end, he told his tired band of followers. Yet again he lectured us about the Vietnam War and his view that an American withdrawal without victory would prove to have dire consequences for Jews both in this country and in Israel. It was a common theme of Kahane's. Indeed, the Rabbi was a man who held strong beliefs and made no bones about them.

Just before the meeting ended, I looked over to Kaufman. He took something out of his jacket pocket and, making sure I saw it, slowly stuffed it back in. It was a fifty round box of 9mm pistol ammunition.

CHAPTER EIGHT

OZ A

The JDL was on a roll and so was I. By the end of May, I was confident that I had been accepted as the person I was pretending to be by the majority of the organization's members. By this time, the JDL had been involved in a myriad of publicity seeking, not to mention publicity-generating, events. Soviet art and photo exhibits had been defaced, exchange concerts had been disrupted by letting loose bags of marbles and, on one occasion, live mice were set free on the auditorium floor. Besides disrupting artistic events, a Soviet airliner had been spray-painted and both Soviet airlines offices (Amtorg and Aeroflot) as well as Palestine Liberation Front (PLF) offices had been taken over and ransacked.

Some arrests had been made, but the criminal justice system of the city was so laboriously slow it was going to take many months, if not years, for those arrested to come up for trial. This lack of effective and timely response by the law enforcement community only served to embolden the JDL's members.

Walking into the office one day, again while out driving my cab, I spotted a bunch of the members, Jansky included, trying on gloves. Since it was nearly eighty degrees outside, my keen investigative instincts kicked right in.

Jansky and the others, very obviously nervous, told me they were preparing to take over the Lebanese Consulate. (There were actually three attacks planned that day. Besides the consulate, one was to be at a PLF office and the other at the Action Committee on American-Arab Relations). They intended to rough up the people inside, take down the Lebanese flag and replace it with an Israeli one. The exploit was to be in retaliation for the recent vicious murder of twelve Israelis, eight of them kindergarten-aged children, by Lebanese-affiliated terrorists who also wounded forty others in the attack. One of the JDL members quietly shared his concern with me over the fact that the people inside the Consulate probably had guns. As the young men were getting ready for the raid, I could tell by their body language and lack of conversation that they shared some real anxiety about this operation. Knowing that I sure as hell didn't want to be a part of this nutty adventure, I drove one of the guys to within a few blocks of the consulate and took off. I also knew I had to get to a telephone quickly and call BOSSI. If those foolish people did what they said they were going to do, someone was going to get hurt.

Jansky continued to be an annoyance. Late one afternoon, a few days after the JDL raid on Arab and Soviet facilities, I stopped in at the headquarters. Three of us, including Jansky, went out to grab a bite to eat.

As we sat around a small table, I could see that Jansky was fidgeting about. Clearly, something was bothering him. Finally, he burst out, "Damn it, Rosenthal, I can't get it out of my mind you're a cop. You look so much like one. You know, after the PLO attack, ten guys went to rough up the people in the Lebanese Consulate but found a cop stationed there. Funny thing, though, before they went, the Consulate was checked out and no cop was in sight."

I had been lifting a spoonful of soup to my mouth when he started his allegation. At that point in the investigation, I had become so comfortable that I really didn't give a damn what Jansky thought. Without spilling a drop, I replied, "You're right, you son of a bitch, and as soon as you're finished paying for your meal, you're under arrest."

The three of us burst out laughing.

Yet it wasn't a week later that Jansky again came after me and in a half joking voice said, "You drive a cab as a cover, but spend the rest of your time writing reports about JDL."

In my report later that day I jotted down those very words. I didn't view Jansky's suspicions as particularly significant. My cover was good, meaning, it was the truth. The JDL knew all about me except for the one important thing I had omitted telling them: I was a New York City police officer.

That same week I was invited to attend an 'urgent JDL meeting.' The gathering was called to take place inside a small synagogue on East Twentieth Street. About three dozen of the most active JDL members were there. Among them were Kaufman, Cohen and his girlfriend Eileen Garfinkle, and Kevin Bendel. Kahane was there to address the group, and I also saw that among the group was Hy Bieber, a bear of a man who was head of JDL security. He was basically a big nice guy who had known Kahane for many years. My conjecture was, he'd been put in charge of security due to his size and strength, not for any experience or background he possessed. It didn't take me long to figure out that the man knew nothing about internal security.

Kahane stood and addressed the assembled gathering. He explained that extremist groups — the Nazis, the Minutemen, the Klu Klux Klan; he named others — were arming themselves in this country and that Jews had to be prepared to protect themselves. He spoke to us about two units being formed within the JDL. Oz A would be the more physically active of them. The individuals in that group would take vigorous physical training and be given instruction in how to handle firearms. Those in Oz B wouldn't be expected to be so involved in the physical end of things, but would take part in more controversial demonstrations than most and be assigned sensitive missions. Three-by-five cards were handed out to those present and we were asked to write down some basic information about ourselves and whether we'd prefer to be in Oz A or B. I put down Oz A, as did Richie Eisner, the other BOSSI assigned officer.

The next Sunday I was home when the telephone rang. It was Kaufman. He told me to get myself over to the JDL office immediately.

Because of the day and time I felt the call to be an unusual one. Not only had I detected a note of urgency in Kaufman's tone but frankly, I didn't trust the man. After he hung up, I immediately called Teddy Theologes, assigned as that weekend's contact detective. Teddy was concerned that I had called him on my home phone right after talking to Kaufman. What if the man called back and got a busy signal? Who would I be calling on a Sunday morning, and why? Fortunately no one in the JDL possessed the necessary experience to apply such a basic tactic.

Because the department didn't wish me to use my car for JDL activities I had to travel to mid-Manhattan by subway. It was nearly half past noon by the time I got down to the JDL office. I didn't know what I had expected to find when I got there, but unquestionably not what I saw. Nearly twenty JDLers were in the main room receiving firearm training from Bendel, who was holding a hi-powered bolt action rifle. I already knew most of those present as they were the most active members of the organization. What I found to be surreal was the fact that a number of them were walking around carrying large caliber handguns stuck in their belts. Bieber had a .45 pistol partially concealed under his jacket, Kaufman a 9mm, which accounted for the box of shells I had seen. I saw another 9mm handgun on a desk top as well as several hi-powered rifles and 12-gauge riot shotguns scattered about the office.

For a moment I didn't know how to react. Bieber and Kaufman motioned me to come with them into Kahane's office where I was to be interviewed for membership in Oz-A. Officiously referring to the white index card I'd filled out a week earlier, Kaufman started off with, "How come you put down you wanted to volunteer to join Oz-A?"

I sucked in my breath. I was just about ready to answer, when, without waiting for my reply, he asked, "Could you kill someone if so ordered?" Again, not waiting for an answer, he followed up with, "Would you be willing to spend the rest of your life in jail if need be?" Almost as an afterthought, he asked, "Could you beat the hell out of someone if so ordered?"

As I stood before these two armed men, I tried to formulate plausible responses to their grade-B movie questions. It would have been all too easy for me, as a police undercover officer, to respond with a 'yes' to any of their wild queries. The trick, I knew, would be for me to show some rational reservation in regard their questions yet demonstrate a sincere willingness to be part of their team.

Carefully, I began, "I don't know how I'd react to some of the stuff you guys just asked. I think I can take a human life if that were necessary. Sure, if the circumstances warranted I feel I could obey such an order." The toughest question of all, why had I volunteered to join Oz-A in the first place, was by now forgotten by the pair. Before I had a chance to respond further, Bieber smiled and said that my answers to their questions were what they were looking for. I honestly believe neither of the two men had any idea how to conduct such an interview and that almost any answers I might have come up with would have sufficed.

Kaufman told me I would be going up to the JDL camp on Sundays as the firearms instructor for Oz-A. He and I would meet the next day to discuss weapon and ammunition purchases. In the meantime, he told me to make up a list of weapons that I thought the organization ought to have. Specifically, he wanted a list of submachine guns, military rifles, handguns, and grenades. Kaufman also told me to buy some gun-cleaning equipment. The JDL would reimburse me.

Bieber took the .45 pistol from his belt, handed it to me and told me to field strip the weapon. The pistol, an Argentine government copy of our military's Colt .45, was fully loaded. I cleared the weapon. Being slightly in shock over the crazy and totally unexpected situation that I now found myself in the middle of, I saw that my hands were trembling, although I did manage to do what he asked. After putting the gun back together I returned it to Bieber, who seemed pleased with my firearms-handling ability.

Bieber and I stepped from the office into the larger room. He called out to Bendel to let me take over the assembled group's training. The other man handed me the firearm, a bolt action rifle. My mind was a blank, having come wholly unprepared to conduct any sort of class. I recall speaking in broad terms to those present about firearms safety, how to check such a rifle to determine whether it was loaded or not, and went on about weapons handling in general.

When the impromptu class ended, Bieber told me to take the two 9mm pistols, as well as the two hi-powered rifles, home for cleaning. He added that he wanted me to make up a firearms training program for Oz-A.

Around 2 P.M. I was driven home by one of the members. When I arrived, I took the weapons from the car, concealed under an old military blanket, and brought them into the house. I recall laying them on the bed and wondering what these people were thinking and what had I gotten myself into. Their behavior and the activities which I had just been party to was completely out of character for the JDL members I knew. It was like nothing I'd experienced in the past and was clear to me that I'd stumbled upon something a lot bigger than the department had envisioned with this group. I picked up the telephone and, for the second time that day, called Teddy Theologes. After relaying the details of that day's dealings I had had with the JDL I believe that Ted, the most laid back of the detectives I worked with and the least flappable, was as surprised as I had been regarding this turn of events. I don't think he, or anyone else in police intelligence, had expected to see this degree of illegal activity coming out of the JDL. To my surprise, and perhaps disappointment, Teddy laconically instructed me to, "Tell the guy (the BOSSI detective at the office) in the morning." I wondered if I had made clear to the detective exactly what I'd seen that day. After finishing my conversation with Ted I set about doing what I had been told by Bieber to do. I thoroughly cleaned the four guns.

The next morning I telephoned Bill Gorman with my report. A half-hour later Bill telephoned my home. He said, "Meet me on Twentieth Street, by Gramercy Park, with all the guns." Once there he'd tell me what to do.

Packing up the now clean firearms in the same military blanket they had come in, I placed the weapons in my VW bug and drove into Manhattan. One of the BOSSI detectives was already waiting for me as I drove up. After a quick hello he told me to stay in the car and that he'd return soon. He picked up the bundle of assorted firearms and headed down the street to the ballistics laboratory, which was located only two blocks away on the eighth floor of the police academy building.

It was nearly an hour before the detective returned. He quickly placed the guns inside my car and told me the guys in ballistics had been upset. It seems my having cleaned the weapons before they got to see them precluded the technicians from being able to run a number of tests on the guns! Nonetheless, all four weapons were test-fired and projectile samples were taken from each. I drove home knowing that I would now have to clean the weapons all over again.

Later that same day, I returned to the JDL's Fifth Avenue headquarters. Kaufman was there, as was Kahane. Kaufman had some business with Kahane, so for a moment he and I stepped into Kahane's office. As soon as I entered I saw that Kahane had a .38 Special revolver stuck in his belt. He immediately noticed that I had eyed his gun. With a concerned glance in my direction, he quickly covered up the weapon with his sport jacket.

Kahane informed me that the organization had been offered a choice of one of six building lofts for use as a range. He went on to discuss training matters with me. The JDL wouldn't be able to fire submachine guns up at their camp because the place wasn't sufficiently secluded, he said. However, selected JDLers would be going to Vermont at the end of the summer. One of the members owned a large piece of property there, where we would be able to use and train with automatic weapons. Kahane added that he would like the organization to procure an M-16 rifle. He also asked me what I thought of one of the members becoming a gunsmith. I replied that I thought that would be both difficult and time-consuming.

When Kaufman and I stepped from Kahane's room, Cohen joined us. We walked into a small side office and I saw that Kaufman was carrying a 9mm World War II era German P-38 pistol, tucked in his belt. Kaufman took the cleaned guns from me and had me show him how to field strip one of them, a 9mm Polish Radom, commenting as I did so that the gun's operation reminded him of how his personal .32 pistol operated. Picking up the pistol, now armed with his newly acquired knowledge, he showed Cohen how to take it apart and put it back together. Kaufman pulled the P-38 from under his jacket and emptied the weapon's ammunition on the table. With those rounds he loaded the Radom's magazine and chamber and stuck that pistol in his belt, telling me to take his P-38 home and clean it.

No problem.

This time, after I left the office with the P-38, I knew enough not to fiddle with it before the gun was tested at the ballistics lab.

On Thursday of that week, using the pretext of returning the now cleaned and thoroughly New York City Police Department documented P-38, I went back to JDL headquarters. This time, among those that were at the office were Bieber, Cohen and Kaufman. According to one of the other members, Kahane was in Montreal and would remain there the rest of the week.

Bieber took the P-38 from me, telling me it was the gun carried by Avraham Hershkovitz. It was the "office" pistol. He went on to explain how all the members of Oz-A had been given a thorough background check. Clearly bragging, he told me that my military and school background had been investigated, that the JDL knew more about me then I did. I silently thought to myself, you poor incompetent bastard. I'd only been involved in this investigation for six months. It was no wonder that, with the level of internal security expertise possessed by the organization, I'd managed to penetrate the JDL to the degree I had.

Bieber continued by saying that the reason the JDL went to such trouble to find out about its members was because, "We [the JDL] aren't fooling around." He added that the organization had people in government posts who were in a position to check on such security matters, and these individuals could even determine if a weapon about to be purchased by the JDL had been used in a crime.

Even if such things were true, which I doubted, amateur that I was, I knew that you never told people things they didn't need to know. The only reason the man went on telling me these things was for the sake of his ego. I nodded my head and tried very hard to show the appropriate respect and awe Bieber clearly felt his words deserved.

Kaufman, not to be outdone, began to tell me that he was in the middle of a deal to purchase Browning Automatic Rifles (B.A.R.) at $150 dollars each. He wanted me to look at them before the deal went down. If they looked okay the organization would buy an initial batch of twelve, to see how we liked them.

Such military firearms were basically light machine guns, weighing in at between twelve to twenty pounds, depending on the version. They were also quite long. I commented, "It won't be easy to conceal the Brownings."

In his distinctive Middle Eastern accent, Kaufman dryly replied, "In guerilla warfare it's not necessary to conceal them." He then told me he would like to get hold of one pound bars of C-4 explosive. Here again, I cautioned him, saying, "That stuff's difficult to properly store."

His answer was, "We didn't want to store it, we want to use it."

I decided to take a chance and asked Kaufman if he could get me a handgun. He told me he'd get me an Argentine .45 like the one Bieber carried. Wanting to see just how good his source for weapons was, I said I wanted a smaller gun, a .38 Special with a two-inch barrel. He promised I would have it in two weeks.

Then, somewhat out of character, Kaufman became talkative. He explained to me how weapons were gotten for the organization. The method was to set up one of their people in a state which had liberal gun laws. That person would find himself a residence, get a driver's license, and register his car there. He would then go to a local gun dealer and buy some weapons, showing that state's identification so as to make the purchases legal. According to Kaufman, the buyer would then take the guns home and store them for a few weeks, in case there was a problem, or in the event someone had somehow become suspicious. Shortly thereafter, the weapons would be driven to New York City.

Kaufman then moved on to another subject. He asked how many rounds of ammunition would be needed for the Sunday training session. He and I discussed what we'd be doing at the camp and decided to buy three hundred rounds of 9mm pistol ammunition, the same number of shotgun shells, and six hundred rounds of 30'06 rifle ammunition. He told me he expected a number of .45 and .44 magnum caliber weapons to be at the camp on Sunday as well. While we were up there he also wanted us to stop in at a small gun store in Ellenville, Dau-Sons, and buy a number of shoulder holsters for the JDL's .45s and P-38s. As an afterthought, he mentioned that he was working on a deal to get 50,000 rounds of 30'06 ammunition for the camp's use.

A few minutes after speaking with Kaufman, Bieber came up to me and asked that I make up a list of weapons which would be most suitable for the JDL to have. I had already given such a list to Kaufman. Obviously the two didn't talk much to each other, but I let it pass, figuring their lack of communication might come in handy some day. He let me know that he had spoken to Doctor Henry Kayman, a dentist. Dr. Kayman had purportedly worked as a government agent and was familiar with counter insurgency operations. I didn't know the doctor well at the time, but he'd soon be playing an important role in the organization's attempts to put together an explosive device. Bieber said that Kayman had told him that dental floss would make a usable baffle material for silencers. Bieber also let out that the JDL had a machinist friend who was capable of turning out the metal parts needed to make such devices — and, by the way, it had been decided that I was to be in charge of all of the JDL's weapons.

Standing with Bieber I thought to myself, here it was June 1st. I'd been appointed a police officer on October 24th, and been a member of the JDL since mid-December. Now, the head of JDL security tells me he wanted me to be in charge of all their illegal guns. Life, I thought, could be most curious.

While in the middle of the conversation with Bieber, Rabbi Pinkus stepped up. I never actually figured out if the man was a Rabbi or not, but Pinkus was one of the stranger hangers-on of the JDL. A bearded man in his early thirties, short and intense, he told bizarre and undoubtedly fanciful stories about his working for some arcane, unnamed government agency. There were tales told by Pinkus of his jumping from low-flying aircraft (without benefit of a parachute, no less) on secret military missions. He told us of the arrest, by his organization, of an individual hired to kill Kahane. Bieber jumped in, saying that the JDL knew of the plot before Pinkus' organization did, and that Kahane was covered at all times.

There was no doubt in my mind that neither one had the faintest idea what the other was talking about. And as far as Kahane being protected by JDL security, that was a joke.

By the time I was ready to leave the office it was already 9:30 P.M. I didn't look forward to the hour-long subway ride home. Fortunately, one of the members, a cab driver, was heading into Brooklyn. A few of us, including Warren Jansky and Adam Kauss, decided to chip in and pay for the fare.

On the way into Brooklyn, Adam Kauss spoke about the organization. A short, stocky man, I had seen him at numerous JDL events. He was like so many of the group's members, a person who was marginal in relation to the larger society: low-income, undereducated, and with little prospect of a decent future. On one occasion, he had told me he took part in two homicides. One was the killing of a White male who had "cut a swastika" in the face of a friend. Kauss told me he was fifteen at the time. The second murder, he said he had been sixteen for that one, took place when he and another young man killed a Black man during a gang fight. Kauss proudly proclaimed that he'd hit the other man on the head with a baseball bat, "...harder than Babe Ruth hit a ball."

Kauss now told his trapped audience that the JDL was the most powerful militant subversive organization in New York City. He knew this was so because the JDL had people inside the government, whatever that meant, who said it was so.

Warren Jansky then once again began to tease me about being an infiltrating police officer, repeating his theory that I drove a cab as cover and spent the rest of the time writing reports on the JDL. I understood the ribbing wasn't just for the laughs he might get. He continued voicing his opinion to the others, saying that I reminded him of a New York City cop, that I was big like a cop and I looked like a cop.

As we continued into Brooklyn I was going to say, "Maybe the organization would have been better off putting you in charge of security instead of Bieber," but I had the brains to keep the thought to myself.

The next evening, I returned to JDL headquarters. It would have been too difficult to justify showing up during the daytime. My reason for coming was to return one of the JDL's 9mm pistols, which I had been directed to clean. Bieber was in the office, as was Kaufman. I saw Kahane also, and figured he must have come back early from one of his Canada trips. Richard Eisner was there as well. Neither Rich nor I were aware the other was a cop. BOSSI never gave the identity of its undercover operatives to anyone, even other undercover officers infiltrating the same organization. I'm sure that policy made excellent sense. There really would have been nothing gained by divulging such information. I suppose it would have also been likely that once officers knew each other's identity they'd tend to socialize. Later, to my chagrin, I'd also discover the tactic was a useful tool of BOSSI's as a means of keeping their eyes on their officers, as each undercover wrote about the activities of the other.

In one of the small side offices I noticed Hershkovitz, Bieber and Kaufman conducting interviews for Oz-A. I killed time with the other members, and when the young man being interviewed left the room, I entered. I handed over the latest pistol I'd cleaned to Kaufman. He took the gun and casually told me he would like to give me his .32 pistol to look at, as he was having some sort of trouble with the weapon. I told him to bring it in and I'd do what I could.

Hershkovitz left the room and came back with another World War II vintage P-38, which he had produced from a small innocuous-looking green bag. He unloaded the gun and handed it over to me so that I could take it home and clean it. With the just-removed ammunition he reloaded the handgun I had brought with me and placed that pistol back in the container.

Bieber wanted me to look at some other rifles the organization had, .44 Magnums, which were not working properly. The head of security let me know that the JDL discovered it could get any type of weapon they wanted from Mexico, but the problem was they couldn't get them across the U.S. border. I thought to myself, "What an insight."

Bieber then went on to ask if the M-1 carbine could be altered to be a machine gun, or if a military M-16 would be better.

At this point it occurred to me that to date, while I had seen a fair number of firearms, the talk of weapons and what would or might be procured was proving far greater than the reality. And what would they be doing with the ones they did have?

With my business finished with Bieber for the moment, Kaufman, Hershkovitz and I entered the main office. I saw a publication lying on one of the desks, *Shotgun News*. The periodical listed large numbers of gun dealers and their wares and seemed to be aimed at the wholesale firearms market. The name on the mailing label was Dr. Henry A. Kayman, with a Bronx address, the same man Bieber had mentioned as having had experience with government counter insurgents. Now I knew where he lived.

A little before 9 P.M., I left the office with Hershkovitz, who carried the little green bag with the pistol hidden inside. On the F train to Brooklyn, he bragged that Kahane had talked him out of returning to Israel as he had planned but instead had him stay around till the end of the summer. Neither he nor I knew at the time that the decision would result in his spending several years in a federal prison.

Hershkovitz told me, in the subway no less, about the plan made a week earlier. JDL members had intended to cause some sort of disruption inside the Lebanese Consulate. He said, "One of the guys had a gun with him. We weren't going to get killed by those Arabs. If it came to that, he was going to kill any Lebanese who shot at us." I was a little surprised by his nonchalance, as if shooting another person was the most natural thing in the world. He added, "And our man was told to kill any witnesses who were in the area as well."

I didn't doubt for a moment that the plan Hershkovitz described was what had been worked out. But it was impossible for me to tell whether this fascination with killing people was simply a sort of youthful bravado, no more then verbalized adolescent fantasy, or the kind of rhetoric which ultimately precedes the violent act so often discussed and talked about among a group's members. Hershkovitz went on, claiming that on the same day there was supposed to have been an attempt to takeover the Lebanese Consulate, the JDL had beaten up several Arabs. He concluded that since no police officers had interviewed any JDL members about the incident, the New York City Police Department was not investigating the matter thoroughly. As the train pulled into my station, I silently reflected on how naive his assumptions would one day seem.

CHAPTER NINE

RACE RIOT

With late June came warmer temperatures, along with shorter tempers. Animosities between already hostile ethnic groups needed only some spark to ignite them.

In the Williamsburg section of Brooklyn lived a mix of poor Hasidic Jews, Blacks and Hispanics. A few years after surfacing from my undercover job, I worked as a Robbery Squad detective in the 14th Detective Division. We covered four precincts, including the 90th, which took in Williamsburg. The place hadn't changed much. Both as an undercover and a detective, I found the area wasn't a melting pot, it was more like a cauldron.

A Hasidic Jew, driving a truck, struck and killed a thirteen-year-old Black girl as she ran across the street. It had been a tragic accident and the district attorney's office released the driver after the incident. They reasoned that there was no way the man could have stopped his truck in time to avoid the child.

Local Black residents did not agree. They expressed their outrage by throwing bottles, bricks and other objects at any cars carrying Hasidic passengers. One young Hasidic child was hit in the head with a rock and had to undergo brain surgery. The situation became more tense. A building was set afire, and Molotov cocktails were thrown into apartments where Hasidic families lived. There were other acts of violence and vandalism. The JDL was called.

It was on a Thursday afternoon when my phone rang. "Come to Ratner's [then a popular Kosher restaurant in lower Manhattan] at seven-thirty. It's an emergency."

When I showed up, there were around twenty JDLers: Kahane, Kaufman, Cohen, Bieber, and Hershman, plus a bunch of other Oz A people, including my fellow undercover officer, Richie Eisner. The Williamsburg section of Brooklyn was less than a mile away, on the other side of the Williamsburg Bridge, just down the street from Ratner's.

Shortly after 8 P.M., with at least another hour of daylight remaining, the JDL group walked over the bridge. The evening was warm, the scene before me unsettling. By the time we got a few blocks into Brooklyn, we saw at least 250 area residents, presumably Hasidim, on the streets. The place was also swarming with uniformed police officers. The situation felt tense.

Bieber told me to stay on the street, he was going to get some weapons. Some time later, he and Kahane drove up in a car. Inside the trunk were five loaded shotguns. Bieber pulled the vehicle into a No Standing zone. Some officers came up and ticketed the car, then asked permission to search it. Kahane told them, "No."

There was some debate between the officers and Kahane, until an agreement was reached whereby the car would simply be moved.

Bieber and the Rabbi drove off.

Around midnight I spotted about fifteen Black men heading our way. I don't recall if they did anything to initiate what transpired next. I do recollect that in a flash two hundred people were chasing them down the street. A fight broke out, with garbage cans being overturned and windows broken. Officers arrested four of the Jewish area's residents. Things quieted down for awhile.

The next evening, I once again ventured into that neighborhood. I saw nothing of a serious nature take place, but my night would have been much more interesting had I been with Kahane. The Rabbi, I later learned, along with Bieber, Kaufman and another member, went into the Hispanic section of the neighborhood. It seems that Kahane had heard there had been threats made: if he or the JDL ever came back into Williamsburg, they'd be sorry.

Kahane was many things, but a coward he wasn't. He and the other JDL members with him walked into a Hispanic social club. They sidled up to the bar, where Kahane ordered, "Beer for the boys."

The place grew deathly quiet. The four JDL members drank their beer, paid the bill and left. The short, middle-aged Rabbi left an unstated message: No one threatened Kahane without there being some sort of a response.

The next night I was carrying a JDL .45 that Bieber had given me. I had decided that for me to go into such an area unarmed would have been foolish in the extreme. And I wasn't the only JDL member carrying a weapon. I saw one of the other members was concealing a .32 pistol and Hershkovitz had an axe and a machete with him.

I met up with Richie Eisner. After I showed him my handgun, he decided to stick with me. Only later (actually, nearly two years) did I find out that Richie, in his report the next day, told my BOSSI supervisors that I was carrying a pistol, a little fact which I had decided not to mention in my report! Fortunately for me, they couldn't say anything about it because that would have put me on to the fact that Richie Eisner was an undercover like me.

Although I was unaware of it at the time, one of the JDL members had arrived in the area with fifteen shotguns and eight high-power rifles. The weapons had been salted away in area residents' homes.

I am not, by my nature, a violent person. Yet I have taken a human life. Such actions are sometimes necessary. Now, I know that bringing weapons into such a volatile situation as the JDL did in Williamsburg was fraught with danger. It certainly upped the ante when it came to the possibility of someone getting killed. All the same, those guns were not taken into the area as an aggressive measure. They had been brought in for potential defense, not offense. I felt then, and I feel now, that a person has a right, an obligation even, to protect his or her interests, safety, family, possessions and group members.

I am aware that there is a great and ongoing debate in this country as to what extent citizens should be allowed access to firearms. I have been in law enforcement for thirty years and I do not fear an armed citizenry. Personally, I would not live in a part of the country that did not permit me ready access to firearms. It has been my experience that the function of the police in this country is often to clean up the mess that sociopaths leave. I have observed that our system of criminal justice does little to rein in these individuals until such time as they do serious damage. These people can do a great deal of harm. I do not wish to see justice done after the fact. There is scant satisfaction there. Ask Ron Goldman's father. Certainly, if there is time and warning enough, then a call to the police would be my first action in the face of a threat to me or mine. Otherwise, I'd much rather take care of my personal protection myself.

Over the next couple of days the disturbances in Williamsburg went on, but only sporadically. Kahane and another JDL member had a run-in with the police. In that incident, one of the Black area residents had pulled out a knife on the two. Seeing the man with the blade, Kahane ran over to some officers of the Tactical Patrol Force (most often referred to by the initials TPF, now a disbanded unit). He demanded the officers arrest the man with the knife. They refused and one of the JDL members began to curse at the TPF members for their inaction. The officers attempted to arrest him. Kahane pulled him away and yelled for him to run.

That act didn't sit well with the TPF officers, a unit whose members at that time were not known for their kind and gentle dispositions. Both JDL members were taken into custody, but not before Kahane was hit over the head with a nightstick by one of the officers, who asked the Rabbi just before he struck, "Remember me?"

At a later news conference given by Kahane, he claimed the officer was the same man that had yelled, "Get the kikes," at a fracas which had taken place that winter involving JDL members and members of the TPF assigned to guard the Soviet Mission.

When Kahane was brought into the station house he found the other JDL member handcuffed to a chair, being beaten by a TPF officer. Kahane shouted, "You touch him once more and you'll be sorry."

The officer stopped.

Kahane was not a physically intimidating man by any means. But he was strong willed, determined, and a forceful leader. Even his adversaries recognized those traits in the man.

CHAPTER TEN

SUMMER CAMP

Just before the season's start of Camp JeDel, I met with Dave Sommer. He wanted me to bring up from the city half a dozen .22 rifles, as well as the same number of hi-power long arms and riot shotguns, plus 10,000 rounds of ammo for each weapon. With fifty campers projected to attend the facility, that amount of ammunition would be expended fairly rapidly.

I left my home in Brooklyn shortly before 6 A.M. and headed for upstate New York. By now, due to my having attended a number of Oz A training sessions at the place, I had been there enough times so finding the location wasn't difficult.

Turning off the main road, I passed two teenagers at the camp's entrance. I was later told that the front gate was secured this way twenty-four hours a day. The sentries, I guessed, were about thirteen years old.

My little white VW bug bumped along the dirt road leading up to the camp proper. After a half-mile or so, I came to the buildings which comprised what structures there were on the camp property — one large building and a dozen or so satellite cabins. It was a weather-worn, ramshackle operation. I doubt if any maintenance had been done on any of the buildings in years. No wonder the JDL could afford the place. It seemed to me that staying in any of the cabins was little more than sleeping in a tent with hard sides, and was clearly only possible during the warmest months of the year.

A quarter mile to the rear was an empty and cracking cement swimming pool surrounded by a wild jumble of growth of all sorts: cat briar, poison ivy, ironweed. I had no idea when it had last contained water, but it certainly was in no condition to be used for swimming when I saw it. It did, however, make an excellent pit for the throwing of Molotov cocktails.

There were seven squads of campers on that first day. I counted nearly sixty in all. They were mostly teenage boys, but I did notice a few girls in the group. These were among the same young people — along with their parents

— that I'd seen Sommer interviewing at JDL headquarters a month and a half earlier.

Cohen took me into the main building. It would be where staff lived, where I would spend the night, and where the camp's "arsenal" was located. The weapons were stored in a room secured by a hasp lock. Only Sommer, one of the other adult instructors, and I had keys to the place. Looking around I counted eight .22s, eleven riot shotguns, four .22 pistols, as well as a .25 and .32, and a double-barrel 12-gauge shotgun that was Cohen's.

Cohen was especially proud of this shotgun. He had had the tubes cut down and told me he thought it was "sawed off," hence an illegal weapon. I examined the piece and asked for a ruler. We found one, and I determined that as the barrels were over eighteen inches long the gun was perfectly legal. Cohen seemed disappointed, saying he'd like to remove at least another four inches from the muzzle and cut off the stock just beyond its pistol grip.

Later that day I spoke with both Cohen and Sommer. Sommer complained to me that he didn't like the idea of having the unregistered, hence illegal, handguns up at the camp, but Kahane had overruled him on the issue. Eyeing the .45 on my hip, he casually commented that it was one of the guns he had gotten for the JDL.

Walking about the place I chatted with a number of the JDL members who I knew. There was something that Cohen had told me earlier that I wished to confirm, that Kaufman had gone to Israel to try and get a quantity of Uzi submachine guns to bring back to the states. It was always hard for me to know just how accurate such tales were. Indeed, between stories of murder, .50 caliber machine guns mounted on motorcycles and rightist plots to exterminate America's Jews, there was often a great deal of verbal debris and hyperbole clouding the issues around me. But in this case two other members who I had talked to that day, independently of each other, confirmed for me that that was indeed the plan. Whether the scheme would ever come to fruition or not I had no way of knowing. Therefore, I put the information into my report.

For the campers, the day was filled with either drill, riflery practice, karate training, or lectures. They were up at 6 A.M. and in bed by 10 P.M. It was a long and exhausting day for the kids. I don't remember ever seeing them at play.

That afternoon was to be my first training session with the youngsters. The seven groups were broken up so that I would be able to deal with a reasonable number of students at one time. I badly wanted to document the number and names of everyone at camp. So I came up with a plan, fully aware that to successfully secure the intelligence I desired in that crowded environment, I would have to implement it in front of everyone's eyes.

As I stood before each succeeding group of students, in my most authoritarian voice I barked out orders: "Take a target!" The kids would each pick up a bull's-eye paper target. Then, "Fill out your names, last name first, and whether you're left or right handed!"

I dutifully had each of the students fire at their now signed targets, after which I collected them.

At the end of the training session I grabbed an old wooden chair and found a spot on one of the cabin's porches, in full view of the camp. Enjoying the warm afternoon summer day, I carefully recorded each of the campers' scores beside their names on lined sheets of paper. To anyone watching, I must have appeared to be a most conscientious firearms instructor. By Wednesday of that week BOSSI had a list of everyone who was staying at Camp JeDel.

The pattern would be the same for the remainder of the summer; up early on Monday mornings to make the three hour ride. As soon as I arrived I'd inquire of Cohen and the others as to what was new. After collecting whatever intelligence was related to me, I'd conduct some firearms training and partake in whatever activities were being offered while I was there. In fact, it was an enjoyable time.

The second week I was up at camp I attended an evening lecture given by a man with a British accent who called himself George. He gave us all a talk on the Urgun and the Stern Gang, military irregulars who fought for the independence of Israel during the 1940s. To the British occupiers of Palestine at the time they were considered terrorists. Thus, many of those who were caught were hung.

Truly, I thought, one side's terrorist is another's patriot.

One of the campers asked George his thoughts on the position modern day American and English Jews faced in their respective countries today. George replied that the situation was analogous to that of the loyal German Jew of the 1930s, who exclaimed, "I'm a German, I love my country!" as they pushed him into a gas chamber.

George's response to the question reflected an attitude and perception I had heard voiced many times over among those within the JDL. I found that the people who spoke these words were xenophobes. Once out of an environment they were comfortable with, they felt as if they were among the enemy. All non-Jews were suspect. People who lived outside the New York City area were suspect. If someone didn't like them, it wasn't because of something they had done, it was anti-Semitism. The world was out to get them and they were only safe among their co religionists in this country, or in Israel. For proof of the peril they faced, they offered the racist handouts they'd collected from various hate groups. They fervently believed that the Nazi party in New York was a threat — all fifteen pathetic members whose leader, according to a BOSSI detective, was a forty-year-old man who slept in the same bed as his mother.

That evening, after the larger group had dispersed, members of Oz A held a special meeting. The person who led that discussion was Frank Laskof, a full-time karate instructor at the camp. He told us that there would soon be classes held for Oz A members on the making and using of booby traps, urban and guerilla warfare tactics, the making of Molotov cocktails, as well as other similar subjects.

According to Laskof, part of Oz A training would include nightly maneuvers. He didn't explain why all this was being done, and I didn't ask. After all, hadn't we just been told we'd soon all be heading off to extermination camps?

After the group broke up, Laskof and I spoke privately. He confided in me that Kahane had told him there was a good chance the JDL would be able to secure a quantity of Uzi submachine guns from Israel. The plan was to have the firearms shipped to this country in crates marked as containing religious articles, specifically Tefillin, small leather-covered boxes containing Hebrew scripture and used in prayer ritual. The scheme was to hide the guns in strategic synagogues around New York City, in the same storage closets where religious materials were kept.

I wondered out loud just how it was that all these weapons were going to be coming our way. Laskof answered that the Israelis owed the JDL a favor. During the raid on the Palestine Liberation Front (PLF) offices a few months back, those involved grabbed many documents before departing. Some of the papers contained the names of PLF leaders who had been placed in American colleges, as well as important people in the organization who were working within the U.S. and other countries.

Kahane, according to Laskof, also directed him to see to it that Oz A members received more specialized training in firearms than the other campers. Therefore, next week I was to bring up with me the JDL's 9mm pistols. Laskof explained that he wanted me to teach the members hip shooting with those firearms, a type of training which he referred to as "pure combat shooting." I had no problem with such a request. Hip shooting was, and is, TV and movie stuff, less than useless except for targets at arms' length distances. In parting, Laskof assured me that Bieber was working on a contact to get M-1 carbines.

Well, it looked to me as if we'd soon have enough guns to fight quite a war. All we needed were some enemies.

CHAPTER ELEVEN

THE WEAPONS CACHE

Although I was now a trusted member of the organization, I had never been told the address where all our weapons were stored. From the slip of the tongue made by a young JDL member, when a group of us were heading up to the camp one day before the summer season, I knew they were being stored at the Hershkovitz home. But I didn't know where that residence was.

On Thursday morning, July 16, 1970, I called in my report as usual. Bill Gorman took the information. After I finished (I hadn't had much to say that day), Bill told me to go to the JDL office.

I tried to explain to Bill that as I had no real reason to do so, I was concerned that it might seem out of character. But he was adamant, which was somewhat unusual for him. In fact, most of the time my police supervisors had to try to keep my enthusiasm for the job under control. At any rate, Bill firmly directed me to head over there. It would be left up to me to come up with some reason to show up.

Known at the time as an upscale sporting goods store where one might be outfitted for a safari in Kenya, Abercrombie and Fitch was located in mid-Manhattan. Their prices were, for me at any rate, astronomical. However, the firm was running a sale that week, advertised in the New York newspapers. There was one item that caught my eye. It was an air gun target which had little colored lights above the impact area, designed to display where one's pellet had struck without having to bother to look at the bull's-eye. It was, as I recall, a thirty-dollar gadget reduced to only five dollars. How could I resist?

So, after finishing up with Bill I set out for the store to purchase my alibi.

With my excuse in hand, I then made my way over to the DoJo on 42nd Street. Just a half a block from the JDL office, I bumped into Hershkovitz and his wife. We all stopped to chat and I innocently asked, "Where are you guys going?"

"To the camp," was their reply.

We parted and as I continued walking, an idea began to take form. The JDL weapons were, I knew, at the Hershkovitz residence. But the couple was now headed two hundred miles upstate. Cohen had mentioned to me during an earlier phone conversation that he'd like it if I could bring some pistols up to camp with me on Monday.

Someone once said, "Luck is nothing more than preparation meeting opportunity." I'd find out soon enough.

Up at the office, I saw that the place was nearly deserted. Hershman and a couple of other members were mostly hanging around, keeping themselves busy with office chores. Without telling Hershman I had just seen the Hershkovitzes, I told the man I needed some handguns for camp for the next week.

"Oh, Jesus, Avraham just left."

I made a minor dramatic scene about how important those damn guns were. I then sighed and said if I had to, I'd pick them up myself.

Without hesitation Hershman gave me his set of keys to the Hershkovitz home.

I then casually mentioned, "I'm not sure where it is."

"Well, I'm not sure either. Call up Bieber and he'll tell you."

That was what I really hadn't wanted to hear. In any sort of professional military or intelligence operation there is a doctrine known as "need to know." Only persons required to have information on a given plan, operation, project, or subject were supposed to have access to such knowledge. The purpose of the doctrine was to keep secure the information which, if the facts got out, could harm the organization or mission. In this case there was no real reason — whether I was a trusted member of the JDL or not — that I should have been allowed to know where the organization's guns were stored.

I left the office, informing Hershman I'd call Bieber after he got home from work. I didn't mention that at my house, attached to my telephone, was a recording device. On the way back to Brooklyn, I walked into a locksmith and made duplicates of the keys given to me by Hershman. There were two for the Hershkovitz place and one for the JDL armory up at camp.

At six-thirty, with more than a bit of trepidation, I dialed Bieber's home number. In as nonchalant a tone as possible I asked him where Hershkovitz lived, explaining that I had to get some handguns from his apartment and bring them up to the summer camp.

Without a moment's hesitation, Bieber replied, "He lives at 1615 Forty-sixth Street. But how are you going to get in?"

"I got the keys."

"Where did you get them from?"

I saw my little plan beginning to unravel.

"Hershman gave them to me."

There was a moment of silence, then, "Good, you hang on to them and don't return them to Ron. I don't trust him."

Sometimes you just gotta smile.

It was still light out when, around eight-thirty, I arrived at the Hershkovitz place, a basement apartment situated in a quiet tree-lined Brooklyn neighborhood.

I first opened an outer door, then let myself into the small apartment proper. As I did so, I found myself trembling with excitement. Following the directions given me by Bieber I walked into the unkempt main room, turned left and stepped over to a table set against the wall. Pulling it back, I saw the wood panel with its two wooden knobs sticking out as he had described. Raising that panel revealed the hiding place. Quoting directly from my intelligence report:

The panel is raised and pulled out, exposing a wall storage area. In this area the assigned observed, 2, Ruger .44 magnum carbines, serial numbers 73405 and 71259, 5, Marlin model 336, 30'30 carbines, new in boxes, a maverick, .45 long colt caliber derringer, serial number 1897, a .38 special S&W revolver, Chief Special, a Radom 9m/m pistol, a Browning model 1922 .32 caliber pistol, a Victor 32 S&W caliber revolver, a .32 caliber revolver, marked Spain on the lower part of the right hand side of the frame, serial number 1862, thousands of rounds of military 30'06 ammunition, M2 Ball, thousands of rounds of .45 ACP ammunition, head stamp WCC 64, hundreds of rounds of 30'30 ammunition commercial manufacture, one box of Super Vel .38 Special ammunition, an empty hand grenade body, 2 cans of Hodgdons rifle powder, BL-C, one can of Dupont IMR-4320 gun powder, 2, 4 lb cans and one 12 lb can of Dupont Hi-Score-700 gun powder, 1, 4 lb can of Dupont, SR 4756 gun powder. Also a quantity of .45 long colt, 7.65m/m and 9m/m ammunition.

There was too much stuff there to commit to memory, so I wrote down what I saw, jotting down as many of the serial numbers of the weapons as I was able. Taking four of the pistols with me, I sealed off the storage area and returned home.

Several days later, when I saw Cohen up at camp that Monday, I told him how I had gotten over to the Hershkovitz home to pick up the weapons I'd brought with me. I commented that it was quite an arsenal stored there. He shrugged his shoulders and told me that I hadn't seen the twenty or so 12-

gauge riot shotguns hidden behind a second false wall in another section of the apartment.

The next morning, when I called in my report to Bill Gorman, he silently took down every word. When I had finished he told me, "Dick, in all my time in intelligence that was the best report I've ever gotten from one of our guys."

His words made me feel very proud. They still do.

CHAPTER TWELVE

GUNS AND BOMBS

In the early morning hours of Monday, July 20th, a two-family home, which housed a Jewish family on the second floor, was the victim of an attempted firebombing. The basement of that building was being used by the JDL to teach karate lessons to local youngsters. Prior to that incident, friction between Black and Jewish residents of Crown Heights, Brooklyn had been high for some time. Beside cultural differences, there was an ongoing struggle between the two groups for both local and federal monies. At the time, various social action programs were being created and huge amounts of government monies poured into urban areas. Since these funds were filtered to the people in the neighborhoods through these social action programs, whoever controlled the programs controlled the checkbook. Money meant power and position — the ability to offer jobs and services.

Indeed, there was so much money being thrown into these areas that it was worth fighting for. Although fair elections were supposed to put community representatives into the available positions of authority, this was not always the case. Intimidation and threatened violence was the order of the day.

One election, marred by such actions, had been ruled invalid by the then-commissioner of the Community Development Agency. It was alleged that men from the Black community had gone to the predominately White Jewish polling places and by their presence and actions kept voters from the area. There had also been reports of ballot stuffing. For the next election, the JDL, its group of supporters led by Kahane, had been asked to come in to protect the rights of the Jewish voters. That election resulted in a majority number of Jewish representatives of that neighborhood's Community Corporation being voted in. Tension between the races had not been eased.

Monday morning I arrived at camp to find the people there highly agitated over the Crown Heights incident. Kahane was particularly incensed.

The JDL had a history of conflict with a local Black activist named Robert (Sonny) Carson. He was considered to be a dangerous man, and some years later would be convicted of homicide and sent to prison for life. But at that moment in time he was viewed by Kahane and other JDLers as the most likely suspect involved in that morning's attack.

Kahane was determined the assault not go unanswered. He told me that he believed it was Carson and his followers who were the persons responsible for the firebombing attack. Still, just to be on the safe side, inquiries would be made. But, should the Rabbi conclude the evidence leaned in that direction, then the JDL would firebomb Carson and his people.

Kahane told Cohen and I that we were to go to Boston. There the head of the JDL was a chemist and the owner of a chemical supply house. He would show us how to make explosives and get us the chemicals we needed to make up additional explosive devices.

Meanwhile the Rabbi directed that Cohen was to start each day at 6 A.M. by having the Oz A group of campers make and throw Molotov cocktails. They'd be tossed into the defunct swimming pool at the rear of the camp. Although these petrol bombs do make quite a sight after being thrown, they only made a dull whooshing sound in the swimming pool. Not that it really mattered. The camp was so secluded that no one could see what we were up to. I never heard of anyone in the area ever complaining about all the firing of weapons we did there.

The talk then turned to procuring firearms. Kahane informed me that the JDL had made a successful contact in Israel for getting hold of some submachine guns. He was uncertain whether the weapons would be the Israeli-designed and -made Uzi, or rather the Swedish-designed Carl Gustaf models, both in 9mm caliber. The Swedish model guns had been long-time standard issue for the Egyptian military. Undoubtedly, thousands of that model weapon had been captured by the Israelis during their various successful wars against that country.

The Rabbi then told us the Israelis (he didn't name names) suggested that an Israeli agent be sent over to this country to set up a manufacturing facility for the Carl Gustaf design.

The idea was not as farfetched as one might suppose. Of all the serious firearms available to military and police units, submachine guns are among the simplest to build. Except for their barrels, which are relatively precision-made metal tubes that must have twisted groves (rifling) cut into them in order to be effectively accurate, the remaining parts are nothing more than some metal stampings and springs. In lieu of screws to hold the parts together, spot welds would do. In fact, submachine guns can be manufactured cheaply enough to be considered throwaway weapons.

At close range this class of firearm can be devastatingly effective.

The conversation ended with Kahane telling me to take back two of the JDL's handguns when I left for the city the next day.

A short time later Cohen and I drove into Woodbourne to purchase the necessary ingredients to make Molotov cocktails. We bought two and a half gallons of gasoline, some soap detergent and a few other items. We then walked into the local sporting goods store to pick up some gunpowder. We were disappointed to learn from the proprietor that due to some new New York State law we couldn't buy any.

That evening and the following morning a bunch of us made and threw Molotov cocktails. I remember the feeling I had at the time, of being involved in a sort of bad boys' July 4th celebration. Once our glass bottles were filled with gasoline and the wicks put in, we'd light the rag and toss the flaming object into the pool. They'd make a satisfying whoosh of flame as the bombs smashed against the concrete. It was great fun.

When I came back to the city and filed my report, the BOSSI people went to work. The whole matter was clearly a sensitive one. They knew about the firebombing, of course. It had taken place in an extremely volatile area. All the targets had been Jews or facilities used by Jews. The police department, and BOSSI, were not about to permit a retaliatory firebombing to take place in the city if they could prevent it. I was told to stay involved in the situation to the maximum extent possible and in any planning which might take place for such an attack.

I had not learned the exact location where Carson and his group held council (the community center where Carson was headquartered was in fact on John Street, in Brooklyn). Nor was I told exactly when the retaliatory attack would take place. But one afternoon Hershman and I were given some money and sent out by Hershkovitz with instructions to buy materials to make Molotov cocktails plus other suitable accoutrements for such an attack: detergent, ski masks, and rubber gloves.

On the morning of July 24th, Bieber, Cohen, Hershkovitz, and Michael Fisher, our karate instructor, who armed himself for the occasion with a 9mm pistol, set out to firebomb Sonny Carson's headquarters. A car had been rented. Then, in order to disguise the vehicle, Bieber removed the license plates from a car parked on the street and set them in place of the rental vehicle's tags.

As Cohen later described the scene to me, they pulled up in front of the place and saw that the facade was made up of two large glass windows with a heavy wooden door set between them. Cohen, sitting in the back seat, had four Molotov cocktails ready to go. Hershkovitz stepped out of the vehicle with a brick in his hand. The plan was for Hershkovitz to smash one of the large panes of glass with his brick, and for Cohen was to heave the firebombs inside.

Hershkovitz was at best a gangly, uncoordinated, and altogether unathletic man. Why he had been the one chosen to throw the brick I never did learn. But, standing before the two large plate glass windows, heave the brick he did. It missed both of his two possible targets and smashed into little pieces against the impenetrable door which was set between them.

Regrettably, it was their only brick.

As Hershkovitz jumped back into the car, Cohen, standing alone in the street, holding a lit Molotov cocktail in each hand, had no idea what to do next. With no target and no back-up plan Cohen could only drop his firebombs and hop back into the getaway car next to Hershkovitz. Everyone then sped from the scene of their "crime." Cohen later told me that Kahane was beside himself at the incompetence shown by his razor-sharp elite troops.

But the Rabbi by then had decided to make up for lost time.

On that Friday afternoon, around 5 P.M., I spoke with Hershman. He had enough sense not to say much over the telephone, dancing around the words and simply referring to a technical problem while telling me what went wrong during the fire bomb attempt.

I wondered if Cohen would be as careful.

That Sunday I called camp. Once I had Cohen on the telephone I first tried to put him off guard by chiding him for not leaving a message for me as he was supposed to have done earlier that Wednesday at JDL headquarters.

I asked him whether we would be going to Boston as planned in order to be taught how to make explosives. He responded, "The message is, it's off."

I was somewhat frustrated by the news. "It's off, we're not going?"

"Yeah, I'll talk to you about it tomorrow, okay, you know I don't want to talk about it...."

But it was my goal to get him to say as much as possible for the recorder. "You don't have to go into detail, because we didn't mention anything, have we?"

"Yeah."

"So, it's off. Period."

"Yeah, there's a replacement. That's scheduled to come up to camp."

In a confused tone of voice, I replied, "Oh, it's coming up to camp?"

"Yeah. It's a possible replacement that one day maybe is going to come by the camp, and stay for maybe an indefinite period of time. For that reason Meir doesn't feel, uh, you know, uh, the other is necessary." Here he was informing me that an individual would be showing us how to build explosive devices right up at the camp. "I'll talk to you tomorrow."

Trying to keep the conversation going, I asked him how the planned importation of automatic firearms was going.

"They're, they're still in, you know, I mean supposedly."

After more discussion about the new firearms and the amount of ammunition available for the pistols, Cohen dropped a small bombshell on me when I innocently asked, "Um, you want me to pick up anything while I'm ... before I come in?"

"Hmm, um, hmm, yeah."

"What?"

"Um, eight-inch pipes, with two caps, with three-inch diameters. Go to a machine shop or something, you know, get them made up."

I couldn't believe my ears. Instinctively I asked, "Now say that one more time?"

"Eight-inch pipe in length."

"Eight-inch."

"With a three-inch diameter, with caps."

"Caps?"

"In other words, caps that can screw on or something, or at least, at least, one cap that can screw on."

"Where can I get this stuff?"

"Go to a machine shop."

"Eight-inch pipes, that sounds like, um..."

"Yeah, well whatever it is."

"That sure does sound like it, yeah."

Cohen was laughing. "Yeah."

Emboldened by the turn of the conversation, the man was in effect freely discussing the procurement of bomb components, I asked him about the JDL's abortive firebombing attempt.

"I hear that you had a problem Thursday."

"Avraham fucked up."

"I don't understand, did you guys try?"

"Yeah"

"You actually threw?"

"I'll talk to you tomorrow, okay? It's one day you know, twelve hours…"

Trying to keep the conversation going, I continued, "All right. Um, Hy has some ideas for next week and he wants me to be involved in it. Is that why you want the pipe?"

"That's why I want the pipes."

I laughed as Cohen continued, "And, and, like, it's going to be very interesting, you know, so, um, you know, just come on up. And bring some heavy motor oil also. Also, make sure you bring that book."

He was speaking about a military handbook on the making of explosives in the field using improvised methods, which I'd borrowed from him.

Realizing that the pipes he wanted me to get were for bombs, and my procuring them could well lead to a claim of entrapment, I decided to come up with an excuse not to pick them up.

"Yeah, yeah, and I can't get you a pipe, man, I mean we got to get that some place around the area. I'm leaving early and I'm gonna hit traffic."

"Yeah?"

"I can't, how can I do it, Stuie? I got to leave early to get up there on time. We'll look around Woodbourne for it, okay?"

"All right."

Later that night, actually it was around one A.M., Bieber called me at home. He said he needed some weapons and ammunition taken up to camp the next day. But, the real reason for the call at the odd hour was that Bieber was upset over an incident at camp. Three of the young people, including one of the instructors, decided that the JDL wasn't active enough for them. They had attempted to steal ammunition and were caught. As they were all members of Oz A, Bieber was concerned he'd have to start the organization all over again.

After a short discussion about what was happening to the planned arrival of submachine guns from Israel, I unsuccessfully tried to steer Bieber onto the subject of the status of the bombing attempt at Sonny Carson's headquarters, still attempting to pin down the time of the next try for the benefit of my BOSSI detectives. Finally we chatted a bit about looking for good candidates for Oz A. The conversation ended with my promising to be over at the Hershkovitzes that morning to pick up the needed guns and ammunition.

At 7:15 A.M. I knocked on the couple's door. The two were still in their nightclothes and I was invited inside their cramped quarters. Instead of opening the wall cover I was already aware of, another secret compartment, on the opposite wall, was unlocked. Inside were additional weapons and ammunition. I took five high-powered rifles along with several hundreds of rounds of ammunition from them.

Three hours later, with my little arsenal safely secreted in my VW, I drove onto the JDL's camp compound. The first person I spoke with was Cohen, who told me that Kahane was really upset over the mess up. Because of how it went down, it had been determined that next time a real bomb would be used. The new plan, as I understood it, was to use the services of some guy named Dov. According to Cohen the man came with the highest recommendation. That is, Hershkovitz had bumped into the guy while eating in a Borough Park falafel joint and recruited him for our purposes.

Dov had told Hershkovitz that he had been a former Israeli commando as well as an explosives expert. He would be at the camp the next day and would instruct us on how to make the needed infernal devices. Now maybe we'd get someplace.

Who knew?

Cohen walked over to the rickety bureau in his room, pulled open the top drawer and took out a clipping from a Black Panther Party leaflet. It was a description of how to make a pipe bomb. This was going to be the plan we would follow in order to manufacture the device to blow up Sonny Carson's community center. So, as we were now into bombs, Cohen, Fisher and I jumped into a car and headed off to purchase bomb making supplies.

After several weeks at camp, both Cohen and Fisher looked more like Third World guerilla fighters than nice Jewish boys. My appearance wasn't too bad. I was a big guy at around two-twenty, with clipped hair and sporting a reasonably clean shirt and dungarees. But Michael and Stuie were another matter. Their hair was uncombed and overly long, with Fisher sporting a thin wispy beard the same reddish brown color of his regular hair. Both had on military green outfits, Cohen in an Army surplus fatigue jacket, both complete with web belts, military sheathed knives and combat boots. Topping off their ensembles were small yarmulkes affixed to the tops of their heads with hair pins. The Catskills had seen many thousands of tourists over the years. But those two guys didn't look like anything anyone had ever seen in this rural part of New York State before.

At first, our little shopping trip went okay. We bought an electric drill as well as the correct size bit needed to put a hole in the ends of our pipe bombs and insert the fuses. We also picked up some heavy duty motor oil (I never did figure what we were going to do with that stuff, but I wasn't all that good at bomb making anyway), also Tampax as well as soap flakes for the Molotov cocktail mix.

But what we really needed were pipes. We decided Woodbourne was too small a town in which to find such exotic materials. So, it was off to the Monticello Supply Company.

The store was pretty large, probably serving as the central plumbing supply source for the area. Once we walked in the door you could hear a pin drop. I guess we didn't look like local plumbers either. Sauntering over to the store's sales counter Cohen did the ordering. Attempting to act nonchalant, Cohen looked around as if he were trying to remember just what it was that he was there for.

"Uh, let's see," Cohen's lips twisted pensively. "I'd like, uh, oh, ... three pipes."

"Three pipes?" the counterman repeated.

"Uh, yeah. About three inches in diameter."

"Yes?"

"Yeah, that's about right." Cohen shifted from one leg to the other, his eyes searching around the store as if he was digging into his memory for the reason he was there. "And around eight inches long should do." A short run job, perhaps?

"Eight inches, huh?"

"Yup. Oh," snapping his finger, a fretful look on his face when he realized that he had almost forgotten something, "And, uh, six caps. You know, threaded caps."

"Same size as the pipes?"

"Uh, yeah."

The counterman disappeared to the rear of the store. We stood around, trying very hard to appear casual, staring back at all the people who were staring at us.

Finally, after several minutes, our three pipes and six caps appeared. Cohen gave the counterman the name of "Wiener" and the camp's address for the receipt. I figured that would cover our tracks for sure. As we were about to leave, a little old lady came up to us and asked, "Are you the boys making the bombs?"

We picked up our things and left the store without additional comment. Three years later, when Alcohol Tobacco and Firearms agents came to the store, to search for the paperwork for the pipes, the very same man was working the counter. "You want to know about the three young guys who came in to buy the pipe bombs?" He remembered every detail of the transaction.

Back at the camp, we stored our pipes in the armory. A new fellow had shown up. Introduced as a Vietnam vet, he had volunteered to show us how to make napalm. So, we all walked back to the charred hole in the ground that had once been a swimming pool and poured Ivory soap flakes into gasoline, heating the concoction over a low charcoal broiler flame (Don't try this at home, kids).

After working up a batch of this stuff, our little gang took a lunch break. While eating our bologna on white bread sandwiches, we discussed putting together a sort of mass production still for making the napalm. Fortunately, nothing ever came of that project but talk.

When the mix became sufficiently gelatinous, we poured the concoction in some bottles and had a good time tossing the lighted firebombs into the blackened pit. Except for the little added stickiness of the mixture, I didn't see any big deal in how this napalm stuff worked over just plain gasoline.

The next day Dov showed up. Cohen and the others had been anxiously awaiting his arrival. They were all under a lot of pressure from Kahane to deal with the Crown Heights situation and Dov was the only hope they had of making a working bomb any time soon.

The man was about five-eleven and pretty beefy, sporting a double chin. He didn't look much like a commando to me, but then, what did I know. I never did learn his last name; in fact, I never even found out if his real name was Dov. From the start I don't think any of us were thrilled with this guy. He came off as a bit too arrogant and self-assured. Now, if he could really do what he said he could do, that would have been different. The man told us he had been instructed to show a small number of those at camp how to make and use explosives. According to him, Kahane had also told him to make us a time bomb.

Cohen, Dov and I walked the rear of the camp where a suitable site was chosen to conduct this training as well as to set off the explosives. I had a 9mm pistol with me. Dov told me to show him what I could do with it. I pointed it at a piece of wood sitting upright against a tree. In the middle of the wood was an oblong two-inch cut-out section. I told him that's what I was shooting for, which it was. I put all the slugs through the hole without touching the surrounding wood. Dov arrogantly informed me I'd just missed. He was wrong and had now pissed me off.

He asked for the pistol and started blasting away. The guy wasn't hitting much of anything. This was our Israeli commando?

For the rest of the afternoon, Dov demonstrated nothing more than how to make Molotov cocktails using the very old hat Ivory Snow (99 and 44/100ths % pure, you know) and gasoline mixture, which we'd been using for some time already.

I left late that night.

It was clear from all that was going on around me that a bombing was going to take place at Sonny Carson's community center in Brooklyn. It was just matter of when. The biggest problem, really the only one preventing immediate action, was that the JDL didn't possess a working explosive device.

But they were trying. Before I had left, Cohen asked me to call the headquarters on Wednesday and tell them he would be coming down on Thursday, that that would be a good time to do in the community center. I made the call.

I had wanted to speak to Bieber and Hershkovitz but it was Nancy Hershkovitz who answered the telephone. She explained that everyone who would have normally been in the office was out, trying to buy a Soviet-owned forty-plus-room mansion which sat on thirty-six prime acres on Long Island. I had heard of the scheme earlier from Hershman. The Russians weren't paying any property tax on this large estate, claiming it was a satellite of their consular offices and thus, being Soviet territory, not subject to local taxation. The powers that be in Glen Cove disagreed, claiming that a significant amount of back taxes were due the town.

I doubt if the Glen Cove government people were actually serious with their threat to seize the house and property for back taxes. I suspect it was simply a move to put pressure on Washington for some relief from having large sections of valuable property off their tax roles. But Kahane knew a good story when he saw one. He publicly announced that the JDL would show up with a check and moving van on the day of the tax sale, and buy the place outright. The JDLers, check in hand — the account had virtually no money in it but, they figured, why quibble over such details — arrived in a rented U-Haul truck. It didn't matter that the sale had been canceled because of pressure brought to bear on the Glen Cove mayor by the State Department. The fellas decided they'd still try for some publicity.

All they managed to do was paint *Am Yisrael Chi* (Let my people go) on the estate's high, stately red brick walls and repaint its mailbox, changing the address on it to, "New Home of the Soviet-Jewish Government in Exile." Some passerby, seeing the hijinks, called the police and four of the JDLers, including Kahane, were arrested. They were released when the Soviets refused to press charges.

Nancy asked if I'd come in and assist her with getting out the JDL newsletter. I needed little excuse to get over to the office. It was imperative that I stay on top of a situation that could well mean the loss of life if left unchecked.

By the time I arrived it was around seven-twenty. Inside was Avraham Hershkovitz and Hershman. Cohen walked in a half-hour later, carrying a loaded 9mm pistol in his fatigue jacket pocket.

I played at helping out with the newsletter for a while, then got into a conversation with the guys. Hershman took me aside and told me that although Kahane had ordered Dov to come up with a bomb for the community center, no one seemed to know how long that would take.

Cohen called Bieber's home around ten. It was Cohen's feeling that another firebomb attempt should be tried soon. Bieber told him, "No." The JDL was going to wait for Dov to create a real bomb before another go would be had on the community center. Cohen, not happy with what he was hearing and deeply unsure of Dov's ability to come through for the organization, agreed to meet with Bieber at the JDL office the next evening to discuss the situation.

Cohen hung up the phone and turned to Hershman and me. He again told us that he had serious doubts about Dov's ability to make a viable explosive, particularly one with a timing device. Hershman insisted such a sophisticated device was what Kahane wanted. Listening to the two young men talk, I was uncertain which was more important to them, retaliating against Carson or pleasing Kahane.

I left the office around eleven, figuring maybe we'd try and blow the place up next evening. I didn't sleep very well that night thinking about it.

The next evening, at six-thirty, I returned to the office. Cohen and Hershman were already there. Stepping away from those JDL members who were just hanging around, we called Bieber and were told to pick up a fifteen pound can of calcium hypnole. Things appeared to be looking up.

Cohen, armed with his 9mm, and with me once again packing my .45, headed over to the Hershkovitz place, removed the can of chemical, then drove to Bieber's. During the ride to his home, Cohen told me that Kahane would be going to Israel in a few weeks. He'd be looking for some money for the organization as well as working on his project of bringing submachine guns into the states. According to Cohen, the Rabbi's brother, who held a position in the Israeli government's Ministry of Religion, would assist him in his efforts.

We got to Bieber's place in Queens around 10 P.M. The big man took the can of hypnole from Cohen and invited us into the house. A few minutes later Hershman showed up.

As we sat around, Bieber told us that he would be going up to camp the next day to give the chemical to Dov. Cohen argued that according to the literature on the subject he'd been reading, you couldn't make a successful explosive device with that stuff. Bieber disagreed.

Bieber explained that Kahane didn't want another firebombing attempt at the community center. Instead he wanted a more powerful device planted, a bomb from which everyone could get some distance away from before it went off. With this blast, according to Kahane, the JDL would be making its presence felt.

In anticipation of the bombing, and the resultant police actions that were sure to follow such an event, Bieber said that he'd soon be taking all the guns, ammunition and supplies from the Hershkovitz place and securing the arms and ammunition elsewhere. I offered to help, but Bieber declined, telling me that this time he didn't want anyone to know where the cache was to be hidden.

Bad luck for me I thought, but at least the guy was using his head.

The next Monday I was up at camp by nine-thirty. Feeling adventurous, I rode up on my Suzuki motorcycle, a pretty blue 500cc road machine. The ride was as pleasant as always, but when I got to camp it soon became apparent that things were not going well. Dov was proving to be an expert in nothing more than making and throwing Molotov cocktails.

From talking to the people up at camp I could see that the situation was getting tense, especially so because a synagogue had been firebombed in Crown Heights over the weekend. Dov told people not to worry, and mentioned to me that Kahane had told him the JDL would soon be getting dynamite.

Cohen, meanwhile, had experimented with a number of chemical combinations. When ignited, the more effective ones burned fiercely, putting holes in a galvanized bucket and literally melting any glass containing the material. But nothing could be made to detonate.

While we were pitching our flaming bottles of gasoline in the pool's pit, I noticed a light plane circling overhead. I asked no one in particular what they supposed those guys were doing up there. Without hesitation, one of the young men standing alongside me said, "Oh, that's the state police. They often fly around here when we're practicing throwing these things."

Everyone just kept on tossing their firebombs.

Cohen then decided to try something new. He was going to follow the directions he had read in a military manual for the making of napalm in the field. To that end we went into town and bought several gallons of gasoline along with a small charcoal broiler.

While we were in town, Cohen and I walked into the local gun store and picked up three high powered rifles the organization had ordered. They were bolt action Remingtons in .308 caliber, two with telescopic sights. I didn't notice what was being put on the federal forms when the guns were being purchased, but Cohen later told me that three phony names had gone on the pieces of paper. That federal violation, falsifying the names on those 4473 forms, would come back to haunt the JDL soon after.

By the next day, Dov was asked to leave the camp. Beside the fact that the man couldn't get anything to blow up, he had assaulted a camper during a drill some days earlier. From listening to how the others had spoken about him I figured the guy wouldn't be missed.

The plan to have Cohen and me given instruction on how to make bombs by the Boston chemist was resurrected. I was told that Kahane was going to make the arrangements.

The next day I was up early. The weather was magnificent. A brilliant blue sky with an occasional puff of fair weather cloud rolling by, it was one of those rare summer days you never forget. Low humidity, mild temperature, unlimited visibility — on such a day a person felt like they could live forever.

That morning our campers were leaving to visit a neighboring camp. A softball game? Maybe a swimming contest? Perhaps a joint military maneuver using bayonets? I don't remember the reason for the trip, only that four people stayed back, all youngsters. I decided that before I returned to the city, I'd "test fire" the new .308 rifles.

I casually walked to the rear of the property and fired half a dozen rounds from each of the rifles. I then carefully placed the empty shells in envelopes I'd brought with me for that purpose, each marked with the serial number of the rifle those particular shells had come out of. Taking the rifles back to the armory, I stuffed the envelopes, along with their shells, safely in my pocket. Had any of those weapons ever been fired in a crime, and their shell casings left behind, there were some people who would have a great deal of explaining to do.

With no one of importance around, I did a full inventory of the armory, noting down the serial numbers of the dozen or so firearms stored there. By now really emboldened, I went into Cohen's room. There I recorded the names of the assorted books on explosives he had lying about. All of them had come out of our own government's printing office: *Guide to Viet Cong Booby Traps* and *Explosive Devices*; *Grenades and Pyrotechnics*; *Military Pyrotechniques*; and *Special Forces Demolition Techniques*. Also in Cohen's desk was a diagram on how to make a pipe bomb. I made a copy on the camp's Xerox machine and also placed that among my things.

I then mounted my motorcycle and had a marvelous ride back to Brooklyn.

Later that evening I showed up at JDL headquarters on Forty-second Street. Kahane was there. Taking me aside he asked, "Do you know what happened the other day?"

"Yeah, Cohen told me a synagogue had been firebombed in Crown Heights."

His brows furrowed. "We have to do something about that. It can't pass. The JDL must take some action."

Kahane then rattled off some questions: "How was the napalm working?" and "Had Cohen managed to make a self-detonating fire bomb yet?" His voice carried tones of both urgency and impatience.

He then changed subjects, telling me he was "obsessed" with a desire to secure a firearms range for the JDL. He handed me a slip of paper with the addresses of several buildings that we'd be looking at as possible sites for ranges. I had been in the office for only fifteen minutes speaking to Kahane when he informed me he had to go to a speaking engagement in Brooklyn. Hershman was in the office and he and I decided we'd jump in my car and go out there as well.

The weather had remained pleasant throughout the day, even in the city, and the warm evening's ride through the light post-rush-hour traffic was a pleasant one. Nonetheless, it still took us the better part of an hour to get out to the synagogue.

Standing around the Hewes Street synagogue when we arrived were a bunch of JDL members, Bieber among them. There was still a minute or two before the Rabbi's talk, and the four of us, Hershman, Bieber, Kahane, and I discussed recent events. I casually leaned back against a car and listened as Hershman blamed the JDL for the latest Crown Heights attack. He argued that we were morally responsible because we had failed to take action after the first incident. Kahane stood there, largely remaining silent. From his body language I suspected he believed Hershman to be right in his assessment of the situation.

After the Rabbi's speech, Hershman and I got back into my beat up VW bug and headed over the Williamsburg Bridge to Manhattan, stopping at Ratner's restaurant. The inside of the restaurant was sort of narrow and long.

I'd never been to the place except with JDL members. It's not that I didn't like the food, I did. Jewish cooking in New York City is really Eastern European cuisine modified to meet Jewish dietary law. Many of the dishes served at Ratner's, I'd eaten only at my grandparents' homes.

We took a seat in a quiet part of the place, it was after 9 P.M. and practically empty anyway, and discussed what the JDL would be doing in response to the Crown Heights attacks. Hershman let me in on how the JDL planned to get itself some dynamite and blasting caps. The organization was going to use a phony building contractor's license to legally purchase this highly controlled material. And, I was assured, a real explosives expert, not Cohen, would be the one to make the timer for the next device, a guy who had told Hershman he had shot and killed four men with a .45 while working for an unnamed U.S. intelligence agency. That would be Kayman, whom I would get to meet the next day.

CHAPTER THIRTEEN

WIRED

On the morning of Wednesday, August 5th, I was informed by one of the BOSSI detectives that starting that night I would be wearing a body transmitter. In police parlance, such a device is called a "wire." Back then, the unit used by the department was always referred to as the "Kel," the name of its manufacturer.

The quarter watt transmitter was perhaps half the size of a pack of cigarettes, although considerably heavier in weight. At the time, these units must have been the state of the art in surveillance and intelligence gathering equipment.

During this period in the investigation when I was to be "wired up," just before I'd go out to the actual assignment, I would meet up with a detective. It varied from day to day who would be there to assist me and where we'd meet. The Kel would be attached to the front of my body, just below belt level, with white medical tape. The on/off switch would be taped open or shut as required. The long antenna wire/microphone combination would then be run up my chest, underneath my tee shirt. The same sticky white tape would be used to keep the antenna wire in place. When the tape was removed at the end of the day a goodly amount of body hair came off with it.

There were two other components used in conjunction with the Kel transmitter: A receiver, usually situated inside a vehicle, was monitored by detectives. Attached to the receiver was a recording device.

It was my experience during the investigation that the sending units then in use had very limited range. I didn't realize this until some time later, when I was put to the task of transcribing the tapes of my clandestinely recorded conversations, a terribly tedious job. I suspect a quarter watt unit, like the one I wore, had at best a usable line-of-sight distance limit of several hundred yards. That is, if the person operating the receiver could see the person wearing the Kel, and they weren't more than a block or so apart, the device would work fine. But that would be under "normal" conditions. When near, or worse yet, inside concrete and metal reinforced structures, the utility of these devices was marginal. The heavy material of such structures, especially those being surrounded by metal, seriously interfered with the function of the Kel.

On the other hand, when out in more open territory, or when in a residential area made up of single-family wood-frame homes, I found that the little devices worked just fine. Years later, I had occasion to be the detective responsible for fitting undercovers with their Kels, as well as acting as their back-up. Knowing the limitations of the devices, I made it a point of getting as close to the officers as possible. Sometimes this meant sitting in a busy restaurant, little more than twenty feet away from the undercover.

The first time a Kel was fitted to me, I began the evening at JDL headquarters. There, in the middle of Manhattan, I was inside a brick building which had a steel skeleton structure. Reception was poor. I had no idea where my back-up team members had situated themselves, but as it was a crowded part of the city I figured they had most likely parked across Forty-second Street, opposite the DoJo. The transcription of that conversation shows that except for some things I said, and a few words from one or two other people, much of the dialogue that summer evening inside the DoJo was so weak as to be inaudible on the tape.

Hershman was there, as were a number of the other members. For a few minutes I chatted up one of the young women who worked in the office, Renee Malkin. She was responding to letters sent in to the organization by people interested in getting additional information about the JDL. I told her that answering such inquiries, "Sounds like a waste of time."

She teased, "Who knows, someday one of these people may replace you?"

I replied, "That is totally and completely impossible."

Hershman and I eventually left for a scheduled JDL meeting which was being held in regard the organization's upcoming Hundred Mile March. We decided to stop off to get something to eat before arriving at the synagogue. My problem was, my police back-up team wasn't aware I'd be leaving the DoJo or, if leaving, where I'd be headed.

I talked Hershman into taking two cars. When I got into mine I carefully repeated which restaurant we were headed for as well as the address of our final destination, Congregation Sichron Moshe, on Twentieth Street between First and Second Avenue.

It was at the restaurant when Hershman told me he figured the Crown Heights bombing would take place sometime between the next day, a Thursday, and Monday evening. I groaned to myself. The surveillance teams were not going to be happy with such a vague estimate.

It was sometime around eight-thirty when I parked my rickety VW near the synagogue and walked over to the group of around three dozen JDL members standing outside of the building. Because the Hundred Mile March, an action designed to bring attention to the plight of Soviet Jews, was a major political event, those involved were drawn from all strata of the organization.

Among the people in the group was Doctor Henry Kayman, a Bronx dentist. "This is our expert," Bieber said, motioning to me with his thumb, his way of introducing us. Kayman wasn't a big man but rather nondescript; a plain dressing guy, a bit shorter than most, wearing black rimmed glasses. You'd be hard pressed to pick him out of a crowd.

Kayman and I immediately began to feel each other out, tossing tidbits of weapons minutia around, to see which of us knew more on the subject. He told us how he could go to Vermont and pick up assorted firearms for very little money. He told us that he could get us .45 caliber pistols, boasting, "You get fifteen or more, they're thirty-five bucks apiece."

Feigning ignorance, I commented, "I thought .45s are hard to come by now." Bieber jumped in, "He can get them."

I turned to Bieber and asked, "How many .45s do you want?"

"As many as I can get."

Kayman interjected, "Thirty bucks apiece. Five bucks more in good condition, forty bucks apiece."

Bieber then started about the JDL's need for an explosive device. "I need a big blast," he said.

Hershman looked in my direction. "Rosenthal wants to go to Crown Heights."

Bieber: "So?"

"In my opinion he's not to go. He's our ace."

"That's true," Bieber replied.

I cut in, "That's ridiculous. A lot of people know as much as I do about weapons."

But Bieber put an end to it. "I need you for more important things. This is nothing. All right?"

To me and the NYPD, a bombing was never "nothing." I was aware that the department had become increasingly anxious over my reports of the JDL's attempts at both constructing a bomb and their desire to blow up Sonny Carson's headquarters. The explosion planned for the community center would have torn the building apart. There certainly would have been fatalities. The friction such an act would have generated between races would likely have had its own tragic consequences. But the head of JDL security was adamant. I was not to go.

Bieber, Hershman and I went back and forth on the matter. All the while Kayman kept on interrupting my arguments with some dopey question about Federal Firearms License holders within the JDL. He needed the license so that he could buy weapons and ammunition for the organization. He explained that legal firearms were far cheaper than illegal ones, and that he could go to Vermont and buy military surplus weapons cheaply, but only if he had an FFL. I turned the talk back to bombs. "We were trying to make cocktails up at camp."

"Well, Dov doesn't know how," Bieber shot back. "But he does."

Kayman saw his chance. "Shotgun powder, calcium hypnole. Hypnole is good. Mixed with pool cleaning compound ground into powder."

Now perking up, I said, "Yeah?"

"About two pounds of that has the power of about three quarters of a pound of C4 explosive. We don't have RDZ or C4 or high brisance stuff. We have low brisance stuff. Therefore, what do you do? You put it into a knapsack, a pillow case or a cardboard box for shaping..."

Trying to sound knowledgeable, I threw in, "A shaped charge. Monroe effect?"

"Right. The greatest mass with the least surface area."

"Yeah," I said, not having a clue what the man was talking about.

Kayman then continued on about a new type of explosive. I wondered to myself if the organization had actually found some sophisticated material to use for the bombing. "We're talking about dynamite?" I asked.

"I've been trying to get it," he said.

"You know where we could get dynamite?"

"Explo Incorporated, up in the Bronx. But you have to know how to use that stuff. It's a shattering load. And like, you can do tremendous damage. I mean if you want to, great, but if you don't want to, you might be sorry later on."

Still wanting to know what kind of person I was really dealing with, I asked, "I got to hear the story about the four guys [the men he claimed to have killed] before you leave here."

"Which four guys? Let's see, there are two guys in Philadelphia, with a pistol. But there were dozens in the Dominican Republic, literally, dozens, including machine guns, carbine, pistol, hand grenade. On one night I even got a guy with a bolo machete.

"What happened was, we had trapped, forty, fifty insurgents. We had 'em, cross fire, sniping at them, but one guy made it somehow, through the cross fire. He started coming up the hill at me, and I'm a lousy shot with a pistol, I admit it, I emptied the clip and that was it. I hid behind a tree, he came looking for me. He had a Tokarev rifle by the way, an old Tokarev rifle, and uh, there there's my friend, half Indian, and he's too busy to help me out, so he hands me a machete and just goes back to what he was doing. I got him with a machete. A bolo machete, two-pound blade..."

"Did you sneak out behind him?"

"No, he came round the tree and, what do you think I'm going to do, I'm not crazy."

"So why didn't he shoot you with the rifle?"

"I was behind a tree, he came around it looking for me."

Hershman and I laughed.

"Don't laugh at me, I did piss my pants, I almost shit in my pants, so it's no joking matter."

He then went on to describe shooting two rioters during a disturbance in Philadelphia in 1964. The conversation then turned back to his working for the government in South America.

Hershman commented, "So you were a professional mercenary."

"No, that's not mercenary, you're working for, you're being paid by the government, that's not mercenary."

Curious, Hershman inquired, "How's the pay?"

"The pay is very good. I've paid off all my debts in one year. I owed my dad for eight years of college. I paid it off in one year. But, what is very, very good is the medical plan."

Kayman once again went into great detail about how to demolish a building of the type Hershman described in Crown Heights. The conversation then turned to simple timing devices using common everyday materials. "Any time you want, thirty seconds to five hours."

Hershman said, "What we're going to have to do is break the window first and place the bomb inside."

Kayman explained how to break out a large section of plate glass without making a loud noise. The conversation then turned to his having a problem acquiring a New York City pistol permit. One of his dilemmas was that his precinct captain wouldn't take a bribe. I couldn't resist, "Nothing more disgusting than an honest cop, you know that?"

On Thursday, arrangements were made for a meeting at Bieber's home in Queens, a single family house set on a pleasant street lined with identical houses. Showing up fifteen minutes early, at nine-fifteen, I parked my little white VW Beetle and made sure I flicked my transmitter on, carefully taping the switch in place.

For a quarter of an hour, while we waited for Kayman, Bieber and I discussed different types of military weapons. When I felt comfortable, I turned the talk to the JDL's attempts at securing explosives.

"Are we getting that dynamite in?"

"We're still working on it."

Still trying to come up with some hard information I tried, "That stuff's hard to find, isn't it? Do you think it can be gotten?"

Bieber mumbled something in response.

"I don't know where you're gonna store it. I can see it in freezers all over Brooklyn."

"It'll be secured."

"And what about caps though? You got to have those things."

"You don't need caps. Good to have them, you don't need them."

The task remained on my shoulders. I had to try and narrow the bombing time line down to a manageable window so that surveillance could be arranged by police. But whatever I asked, however I tried to come up with the information, Bieber answered vaguely. "It's going to come off, but if it'll be Monday or not, I don't know."

At that point it became clear that he didn't know himself.

Then Bieber engaged in some wishful thinking, "Meanwhile, the Carson people are sitting on pins and needles."

I instinctively responded with the truth, "I don't know if they're sitting on pins and needles or not. I don't think they even know we exist at this point, to tell you the truth."

"Really? They found the bricks in front of the place."

"Some schmuck tried to get through a door with a brick. Beautiful."

I turned the conversation to the recent disturbances we'd been involved in in Crown Heights and Williamsburg.

"You had those damn shotguns in the trunk of the car?"

Bieber smiled, "The cops there wanted us to lift the trunk up."

"They asked you to open the trunk up?"

"The Rabbi told them we didn't have a key."

I laughed.

"We didn't want that trunk opened. Comprende? There were four shotguns inside."

"Four shotguns, loaded?"

"Fully loaded. With six [shells] in the magazine and one in the chamber."

"Oh, boy. I didn't understand why you pulled up in front of everyone with that car."

"I wanted them to see it."

"You wanted them to see it?"

"I wanted the Puerto Ricans to see it. You know what would have happened? They would have gone crazy. (inaudible) Puerto Ricans (inaudible) they would have turned tail."

Unable to figure out his logic, I replied, "Yeah, but the cops would have had a conniption fit."

Bieber's premise was irrational. He was saying that he, with Kahane inside, had deliberately parked a car with a trunk full of illegal weapons, in front of the police, in order to frighten away area Puerto Ricans. The fact that the place was teaming with Tactical Patrol Force officers, and he would have had no opportunity to display those weapons without being arrested, apparently had never entered his mind. Reflecting on his words I decided that it was far more likely that at the time he had no plan to begin with and was now simply giving me a bogus reason for what had been a mind-numbingly foolish stunt in the first place.

Kayman arrived. First we unloaded the firearms he had brought from his car's trunk. Two 30'06 Johnson military rifles, a .22 rifle, a .303 British military rifle, as well as a couple of handguns; a .22 and a 9mm Browning Hi-Power. Bieber brought out a 30'06 rifle and a .45 semi-automatic pistol for his contribution to the show and tell session. Kayman spoke freely about how he had acquired his weapons, including his .22 pistol which was stolen.

Bieber turned the discussion to politics. He asked my thoughts on the American far right, and the threat they presented to the Jews in this country. From the type of questions he began to ask, it became clear that Bieber was testing me. I responded as best I could, attempting to sound as paranoid as I dared.

He first asked me about one particular right-wing paramilitary group, the Minutemen. I wasn't all that familiar with them and decided to let Bieber mentor me.

"What's the Minutemen?"

"They're bad. Bad for us."

"They large in number or what?"

"They're large in number, well-heeled. They're well armed and supported by the right wing in the Army. They've got bazookas, they've got weapons carriers, half-track."

"Where the hell do they store all of this stuff?"

"Out west."

Bieber then asked me my thoughts on the status of American Jews. "What do you think the problem is here? In your opinion."

I hadn't thought much about it and I stalled for some time to collect my thoughts, "Mine?"

"In your opinion."

"That we have a problem it's, uh, it's obvious that, uh …"

"You think there's a possibility of this becoming another Germany?"

"It could happen," I said. "Could happen. Don't you agree?"

Bieber did indeed, saying, "The American's penchant for violence is much more than the German's."

"You think so?"

"The rioting during peace time? You never had this in Germany."

Struggling to find something to agree with, I tried, "Yeah, it's … you got to be careful you know. I mean you got to be on your toes. In this country … can't wait till it's too late."

Kayman then offered his thoughts. "A magazine I read had a fictional article, how the army could take over this country … but at the time I didn't know it was fiction. It scared the hell out of me, it was so real, you know, it was so logically planned."

Bieber asked, "Did you read the Minuteman article?"

"No, I never did."

"Last year, in *Playboy* magazine."

Well, now at least I knew where Bieber got his intelligence information.

Kayman responded, "Oh, yes, oh yes."

"They're talking about poisoning reservoirs, they're talking about, uh, germ warfare."

I next asked what I thought was a logical question, "Yeah, but who are they going to fight?"

"The government, if they have to, to take it over. And they're talking about what they're going to do to Jews here. Every lamppost in New York, they're going to hang a Jew from it. They talk about concentration camps."

Kayman, now agitated, added, "They're madmen ... the cops know about it."

So, according to Bieber, the far right in America was in the process of building concentration camps, complete with gas chambers. There was a vast conspiracy, he told us, between our nation's law enforcement officers and the right wing zealots, fully equipped paramilitaries in collusion with the active Army. I just sat and listened as the two men went on.

Bieber's lowered his voice, "I want to tell you something. You know the JDL that exists on the surface. But there's one that don't exist on the surface."

Kayman then asked the JDL's head of security a very good question, "Why are you telling us this?"

"Just to give you an idea that something exists besides what you see on the surface."

I piped in with, "We have an underground unit too?"

"We have an underground unit too."

Kayman nodded, "Very nice, very nice.... As few as we are, as weak as we are, our enemies are less committed to their side than we are to our side."

Bieber replied, "We have no choice. It's a question of survival with us."

Bieber and Kayman continued on about tanks of compressed gases to use as explosives. The two bounced off ideas from shooting at the containers with high-powered rifles to having them cook off in an oil fire. I was getting lost.

"But you know," Kayman suggested. "One guy can carry a SCUBA tank and a tank of oil cut with kerosene. You stopper that with a short little pipe and a long pipe. The short pipe bubbles the gasoline. The big pipe picks up the gasoline and you hope that the oil is heavy enough it goes out quite a distance in front of you."

Totally confused, I asked Bieber, "What do you want to do?"

"Flame thrower," he said.

As Kayman took down directions to camp, Bieber confided to me, "I wasn't bullshitting you. I told you I was saving you for something else."

"Yeah."

"Yeah. This is nothing, this is all, this is all just a warming ... If everything comes through in September it'll be beautiful ..."

I pressed on with, "You keep on mentioning September is the big month."

"Get a passport," Bieber said. "You may need it."

A passport? What was he talking about?

Kayman didn't seem to care, he was excited. "What else can we get? Wash and wear shirts ..."

Bieber and I helped Kayman pack up his firearms and return them to his car. The plan was for me to be up at camp on Monday, where, hopefully, we'd finally get to put together something that would blow up.

Bieber and I stood outside, watching Kayman drive off, when Bieber smiled, "You'll be doing a lot of traveling."

CHAPTER FOURTEEN

NO BOMB YET?

The Monday after my meeting at Bieber's, I got up to camp at about ten. Kayman had not yet arrived. Cohen decided that with some time to kill he'd make up a batch of napalm. He had an Army field manual detailing recipes for various incendiaries and explosives using ingredients commonly available in the field.

With material he picked up around camp, Cohen headed out to our 'official' testing area, the old swimming pool. The Army field manual was quite specific. The first thing that we needed was a double boiler. We didn't have one of those. Cohen did have a small charcoal burner intended for backyard picnics. It would have to do.

He lit the charcoal briquettes. While they heated up, he took some gasoline and filled up a quart size coffee can. When the coals were good and hot, he placed the can on top of the little grill. While he was doing this, he softly talked to himself, repeating the directions. Unless someone looking on actually knew what he was up to, they might have thought Cohen was boiling an egg.

I warned him that what he was doing was not a good idea and stepped back about twenty-five feet.

Cohen, his face squarely over the gasoline filled container, watched the surface of the liquid as it started to bubble. He then slowly mixed in his soap flakes.

I do not know why that container of bubbling gasoline did not explode in Cohen's face. Logic said that it should have. The day was warm and still. The volatile vapors clearly had to have been overflowing the rim of the metal can and coming into contact with the glowing charcoal. Had there been an explosion, Cohen would certainly have been killed. My proximity to an igniting quart of gasoline would not have been far enough away to prevent me from being badly burned. But nothing of the sort happened. Cohen fiddled with this and that until satisfied with the consistency of the mixture, which we then poured into a few bottles, lit the wicks and tossed into the pool. The new Molotov cocktail blend, little more than thickened gasoline, proved to be less useful than the normal product.

I dodged many bullets during this investigation. Confrontations with men who rightly guessed my true identity, inept bomb-making attempts, long hours spent with heavily armed paranoids who hadn't a clue how to handle their firearms, all put me in peril. But I count this incident, this boiling can of gasoline, as being the most dangerous of them all.

At 3 P.M. Kayman showed up with what he called some groceries: calcium hypnole, fertilizer, charcoal briquettes and shot shell primers. It was now several weeks since the first Crown Heights attack. Discussions and planning for the JDL's retaliatory bombing went on and on with no results. Tension within the organization's inner circle was high. But there was equal if not more pressure being felt within the intelligence unit of the NYPD. A bombing was being planned and people were actively engaged in its execution. It was known who and where the target would be, and most likely who would be involved in the attempt. The only problem was, no one knew when the attempt would be made.

What was the department to do? What they did was depend on the information of an inexperienced undercover to give them guidance on how to deal with the situation. Therefore it was ultimately I who came to feel this pressure. The detectives working in BOSSI knew that to push an undercover was to invite disaster. Either the information would be forthcoming from the people within the organization or it wouldn't be. If I, as the undercover officer, were forced to do things that might be perceived as abnormal, for example, hanging out at JDL headquarters long hours for no apparent reason, someone was bound to become suspicious. But the department's hierarchy didn't know, nor I suspect care, about such things. Those in charge simply wanted results. I believe the detectives running the investigation tried to insulate me from this pressure, but I could sense it nonetheless. They certainly seemed more jittery and tense than in the past.

Kayman got out his bag of tricks. He put together several concoctions of his explosive mixture, babbling on all the time. "This is important!" he'd declare. Or, "No! that won't work." At times he reminded me of a medieval alchemist completely lost in his quest to turn lead into gold. Our little band of terrorists managed to ignite the stuff he created; melting a couple of bottles and vaporizing a galvanized bucket. But nothing seemed even remotely ready to explode.

Kayman left at dinner time. He'd come back another day to try again.

Meanwhile, other JDL members were preparing for what they believed would be an imminent attack. Fisher took a 9mm pistol from the armory and an extra magazine. He stuffed the gun in his belt, telling those around him it was what he'd be carrying on the mission. Cohen and Hershman assured Fisher and me that they too would be armed during the assault.

Now, not only didn't I know when the attack would be going off, but I'd be telling my superiors the guys involved would be packing heavy iron. Great.

Around 8 P.M. Hershman walked into the cabin where Cohen, Fisher and I were sitting. He told us that Bieber had called and told him there'd be no bombing attempt that evening — really early Tuesday morning — because they had no bomb.

I went home the next day as was my usual habit. My position continued to be a difficult one. Should Kayman, by some miracle, actually figure out how to make an explosive device, it would only take a few hours for a hasty plan to be put into action. I had to continue to keep in touch with these people, yet try not to arouse their suspicions.

I returned to the office Thursday. Hershman was there, busily preparing for the Hundred Mile March from Philadelphia to Washington, D.C., which was to take place the following Sunday. As it was after six, I offered to take him to dinner. It would give me a chance to find out what was going on without other ears around me.

He told me that he'd been informed that Kayman had actually succeeded in creating a bomb up at camp that day. But he still wasn't sure when there'd be an attempt on the Crown Heights Center.

When we got back to the office, Bieber grabbed Kahane and Hershman and the three men stepped into the Rabbi's office to speak privately. For fifteen minutes they were in discussion. I could only speculate about what was going on, but I had a good idea.

I left for home around nine-thirty. When I got there I decided to call Kayman. One of my favorite intelligence gathering techniques was to ask a number of people about different aspects of the same thing, hoping I'd be filled in without anyone knowing just how much I knew. It was shortly after ten when I turned on the tape recorder and rang him up. Kayman started the rambling conversation by bragging about how his latest device had worked.

"I was up there today. It worked fine. I found out why it didn't work the other day. It was very simple, there was no compression, the gas leaked out."

A bit dubious, I wanted to know more. "Yeah?"

"Oh, well, first of all I got hold of two cans of calcium hypnole today. You know you can't buy it in New York City because it's illegal. And if you're an outside New York City resident you need a special permit. Anyway, I went up to Yonkers, to Visigoth's."

"Never heard of it."

"V I S I G O T H'S. It's one of the biggest places there is. It's huge. And I went in and I got some Blower Z-934, spherical ball. They didn't have any Blower Z-692, and I got some Kermie's calcium hypnole."

"How much of the stuff did you get?"

"A pound can of each. I just wanted a little test, you see. I got the smallest quantity possible, just to see what would happen."

"I thought calcium hypnole was difficult to acquire."

"Listen, you don't look a gift horse in the mouth. I don't know why they sold it to me. While I was there two guys from the Nassau County correctional system, two deputy sheriffs had driven all the way up there to pick up twenty pounds of Z-234. They're reloading their own. Two twenty-pound kegs. One guy was smoking. I asked him, 'Do you have to smoke?' He said, 'Why?' I said, 'My car's parked next door,' He said, 'Don't worry about it.' I didn't worry."

"Yeah, I wouldn't."

"Anyway, what I did was figure some things out. First of all, the way we did it last time, we had put cardboard liner inside the bottle cap so that the heat would not cook off the hypnole, just cook off the primer itself. Second of all, we had a full jar and it was compressed. This is not compressed and finally, we made many, many, I made many, many mistakes in allowing all that exposed flame to play all over to cook things off. But today, no sweat."

I wanted to get some idea of the power of the device. I asked, "Big bang?"

"It wasn't very loud but it was pretty good."

"What did you use?"

"That mixture we made up. I'm very grateful to you for crushing up the tablets by the way."

Some of the chemicals had to be prepared before use, which I had helped to do. But I wasn't thrilled by the way that sounded on the tape. I tried to get the facts straight.

"Oh, well..."

Kayman wouldn't let me talk. He went on, "I made a mix, yeah, three quarters of the hypnole, in other words, three quarters..."

"That stuff you just said I crushed was left over from the batch that you made me crush the other time."

"Fine, we used that. Three quarters of that, one quarter of Z-934 and that was just very sweet. In other words the hypnole acted as a primary inducer, a burster. And when the other stuff went in, it was just fine. Then Stuie and I did it again, then I think we did it a third time. Everything went bang, but nothing spectacular."

It didn't sound like his "bombs" were as big a deal as Kayman was making them out to be. So, seeking some sort of confirmation, I asked him, "Stuie was happy?"

"Oh, Stuie was very happy. Stuie is going to show the boys tomorrow."

Having no idea who or what he was speaking of I asked, "Which boys are you talking about?"

He didn't answer the question, instead he went on about how much of the bomb making stuff he had left up at camp. Then, "I got to talk to you."

"Yeah."

"I can't talk," he said.

"You can talk over the phone, who could be listening at this hour?"

Who indeed?

He then went on in great, boring detail about his plans to make some sort of explosive device. By that time I couldn't figure out what the man was talking about. I was growing weary so I suggested we discuss whatever he wanted to talk about during the Philadelphia rally on Sunday.

While I was confident there'd be no bomb attempt before the start of the next week, and especially in light of the fact that the Hundred Mile March was taking up so much of the JDL's leadership energy, I still thought it best to keep tabs on the key people. So on Friday, August 14th, I gave Ron Hershman a call.

Hershman was a bright, streetwise kid with a sharp wit. The crux of the matter was, I didn't want to have to take a bus to Philadelphia and back that Sunday. Not only would it have been uncomfortable but most likely also unproductive. So I figured Hershman, who was one of the organizers of the demonstration, would be a good guy to hook up with. I first tried calling him earlier in the evening. He wasn't in so I left a message with his mother for him to call me, which he did several hours later.

"Got a message that you called. I decided that I'll call you back."

"That's awfully nice of you. How we doing, Ron?"

"Thank God."

I respond in my best Eastern European Jewish accent, "Tanks God, tanks God."

"Thanks God. Uh, how we getting to Philly on Sunday?"

"Ron, you're renting a car. Remember?"

"I might be staying overnight. If I get a good enough place to sleep. Really."

Seeing my ride go down the drain I asked, "Where does that leave the kid?"

"I don't know. There shouldn't be any problem really, coming back, there's a bus coming back."

"Okay, let me get this straight now. I'm going to come and there's going to be a bus but I'm not going to take the bus I'm going to take the car, but pay a bus fee, right? And then when I come back, I come back in a bus. Except there might not be any room because I went in the car the first time, right?" Not pleased over the thought of being in a cramped bus for the ride back to the city I said, "You're a pain in my ass, Ron. How much is the bus?"

"I think the bus is getting ten bucks round trip."

"So that means, no matter how I cut it I got to give you ten bucks anyway, right? And that'll reserve me a seat on the bus, right? So I can go with the car, right? And maybe come back in the car, but it's not guaranteed. That sounds okay. That sounds reasonable. Who do I give the ten bucks to and when?"

It was just before 7 A.M. Sunday morning when I walked into the JDL office on Forty-second Street. The place was more chaotic than usual. Swarms of people, many new to me and I supposed there only for this event, ebbed and flowed around me. Hershman spent much of his time shepherding the people to the buses sitting at curb side chartered for the trip. By the time the buses left, at around eight, only he and I remained. It was now left to us to rent a car for the ride to Philadelphia.

Hershman had only forgotten one small detail. We were in the middle of Manhattan, it was a beautiful Sunday morning, and hundreds, if not thousands, of other people also wanted a car for the day.

Nothing was available in any of the car rental places we asked.

This left one option open. My VW bug. My old, falling apart, non-air-conditioned rust bucket of a Beetle. I had bought this car from another member of the Air Force a few years earlier while stationed in Germany. I had paid three hundred and fifty dollars for it and had brought it back to the States with me. As the saying goes, the car didn't owe me a dime. Nonetheless, it was very tired. I wondered how I was going to explain to the guys at BOSSI the several hundred mile vehicle expense report which I'd have to submit.

Hershman and I started our trip by heading out the Lincoln Tunnel and finding the New Jersey Turnpike. Somewhere in the middle of Jersey my right rear fender fell off. We stopped, backed up and retrieved the hunk of metal, tossing it on the rear seat. "Gee," I thought, "only a couple of hundred more miles to go."

I needed gasoline. Pulling in to a thruway service station, I filled up the tank. The bill came to three dollars. Hershman paid with a one hundred dollar bill. I guess so as to ensure that nobody would ever remember us.

Somehow, a little after eleven, we managed to get into Philadelphia. It was a hot August day, the sun blazing. I noted that most of the JDL kids standing around Independence Square wore army fatigues and combat boots. They must have been dying in that heat.

Before the ceremonies began Hershman and I found Cohen and Bieber. The planned bombing of the Crown Heights Community Center came up but no date was mentioned. Hershman did argue not to have Fisher there, as he figured the guy was too inept for the job.

Hershman walked over to Kahane and asked him about getting a rental car in Philadelphia. He was given the okay and off he went to find one. Meanwhile, I stepped over to Cohen. He was in full JDL combat fatigue uniform. In his Army surplus jacket he carried a very loaded 9mm pistol. I then saw that one of the other members was armed with another of the JDL's 9mm pistols. He explained he was holding it for Fisher. Cohen whispered to me that another guy was carrying a .45.

I saw that the potential for trouble here was very real.

Bieber, our head of security, explained to Kahane that he had brought along the three handguns, four riot shotguns and a hi-powered rifle. From his pocket, he casually pulled a handful of shotgun shells and some .308 rifle cartridges.

In the mindset of the JDL, we were all now in enemy territory. I'd seen this before with these people. Once out of the city, street smart and otherwise tough guys all of a sudden became fearful. In their minds, far right wing nuts, armed to the teeth, would be lining the march route, ready to do in the JDLers. They truly believed what was written in the hate literature crap they so carefully collected. They forgot that the stuff they were reading had as much truth in it as the nonsense they themselves generated to the media.

Kahane stepped up to a microphone and began to speak, "It is time to take to the streets and plead for Soviet Jews. We are not a respectable organization. Thank God for that because if all the respectable Jewish organizations were laid end to end, there would be no end to them."

The many JDLers in the crowd cheered their leader. It was a good speech given by a good speaker. At its conclusion, the JDL members marched nearly half a mile to a Holocaust Memorial. The plan was to hold a short ceremony before moving on to the camping area at Valley Forge.

Then a most foolish event took place. I suspect that the camp members' proximity to weapons over the course of the summer at the JDL's private upstate New York facility caused them to forget that, to the rest of the world, guns were indeed guns.

I was across the street from the JDL van when I saw one of the members moving toward it carrying a hi-powered rifle resting on his shoulder, the weapon fully exposed. What I didn't know at the time was that Fisher had decided it would be a good time to move these weapons from inside the trunk of a car and over to the larger vehicle. Although the four shotguns were wrapped in a blanket, the kid with the rifle must have forgotten he wasn't still in the middle of camp and simply hoisted the weapon onto his shoulder. The police went nuts. There were several hundred people between me and what was going on but it was clear that some of the JDLers were being taken into custody, among them Kahane.

For some time there was mass confusion. It took some doing but I finally got a ride with another member to the police station where I managed to speak to the Rabbi. He informed me the JDL members were being charged with several offenses, not the least of which was possession of sawed off shotguns. What Fisher hadn't known was that although the eighteen-inch barrel shotguns were legal in most states, including New York, the Pennsylvania minimum lawful barrel length was twenty-two inches.

This whole march had been the brain child of Kahane. He was the person who made decisions on the spot for the dozens of minor emergencies that inevitably cropped up during such an event. That's how the man's personality worked, and he was quite good at it. But, at the moment, he was in custody and basically incommunicado. In the briefest of conversations he told me to get to Bieber and have him take the JDLers on to Valley Forge. The man's instructions were clear, logical and to the point.

As soon as I could get back to Bieber, I gave him the message. All around us were hundreds of young people, milling around in this city park waiting for some direction. They were hot, tired and hungry and the day's light would soon be gone. These youngsters had to be moved out soon to wherever their next destination was. Decisions had to be made, and made quickly.

Even after I told him what Kahane had said, Bieber just walked around in a daze, his eyes looking straight ahead. The guy didn't have a clue what his next course of action should be. I tried to get his attention and asked him what he was going to do. Here I was, the undercover cop, the guy who wasn't supposed to make decisions for these people or get involved in their actions. Now, I was trying to rouse the head of security of the organization that I had infiltrated into doing something!

My position was untenable and I knew it. I took a deep breath, found my way back to my car and drove home to Brooklyn. I left behind a motley, dispirited and disheveled group of young warriors.

CHAPTER FIFTEEN

MORE BOMB GAMES

During the week the JDL was involved in its Hundred Mile March, the long delayed bombing was to take place. On Tuesday, I showed up at the office at 6 P.M., my usual time when just popping in. I was uninvited but deeply enough involved in the organization by this time to get away with just hanging around

Bieber, already there, took me to one side. There was a problem. The head of the summer camp had told him that federal agents had made inquiries at the local gun shop where several rifles as well as ammunition had been purchased. It seemed that the high-powered rifle confiscated by the police in Philadelphia was one of the recent acquisitions made by the JDL at that store, one in which the federal firearms forms had been falsified, a serious offense. Bieber figured all he could do was wait and see what transpired. Well, I guess that was a plan of action.

Hershman came in shortly before eight, carrying a pair of gloves (it was August) as well as a license plate, the number of which I memorized. The plate was stolen and the intention was to put it on the car he had rented in Philadelphia for use during that night's bombing.

A quarter of an hour later Cohen, Fisher and Renee Malkin came in. They had just come back from a movie. Malkin, even when she wore her heavy rimmed black plastic glasses, was pretty in a simple sort of way. She wore no make-up and her clothing was quite conservative, her skirts always worn below the knee.

It was explained to me that the plan was for Kayman to show up with his device, then the little group, including Malkin, would head over to their target in Brooklyn and blow the bomb. It would be Malkin who would carry the explosive. She giggled and told me that if she were stopped by the police and able to ditch the bomb, her story would be she was a prostitute. A pretty ironic cover I thought for such a proper and rather shy young lady.

Kayman finally called. Bieber grabbed the phone. We all waited anxiously for the conversation to end. Bieber hung up the receiver and told us Kayman wouldn't get to the office until 1 A.M.

I decided to go home. Not being directly involved in the attempt, there was little more I could do that night. Anyway, to hang around much more would have been strange. As I was leaving the office, one of the older JDL members sidled up to me. In a nervous whisper, he said he thought Kayman was a federal agent. Whatever.

The police put the Crown Heights center under surveillance until 5 A.M. the next morning.

I awoke the next day and turned on the radio. There was no news of a bombing, a bombing attempt or any arrests. I was livid.

At 10 A.M. I called the JDL office. Sheldon Davis answered the phone. He was a young man who was spending more and more time hanging around. I came right out and asked him what had happened? According to him Kayman hadn't gotten to their office until 4 A.M. And he had forgotten a critical part of the bomb. At this point, I couldn't tell whether the man was a genius or an idiot, but I was now leaning toward the latter theory.

The young man went on to tell me that Bieber was going to be in the office at midnight and suggested I come over around 9 P.M.

All this information was relayed by me to the BOSSI detectives. It was decided that I'd be wired again that evening, not that the transmitter had been very efficient the last time I'd worn it while at the JDL office.

I arrived at the DoJo at 9 P.M., my body wire in place and switched on. The first person I spoke with was Renee Malkin. An ingenuous young woman, she talked freely to me about her involvement in the planning and participation in this serious felony. She told me, and the detectives who were listening in, Kayman had sent her to buy some sugar and candles, material to be used in the bomb he'd be making for that night's attempt.

In one of the office's side rooms I spotted a fifteen-pound keg of calcium hypnole, plus four pounds of some other chemical powder whose name was unpronounceable. Cohen's jacket was lying next to the cans, inside one of the pocket's was a fully loaded 9mm pistol.

It wasn't until after midnight that Cohen, Fisher and Hershman walked in. I had to let the detectives outside know who was here as well as what weapons they were carrying. I could only hope the transmitter worked better from inside the office that evening than it had on the previous occasion.

I started the conversation with, "Hello fellas. Welcome to the party." Pointing in the direction of the two others in the office curled up on couches, I said, "Renee and Shelly, they're both asleep."

Cohen asked, "Did Kayman call?"

"Kayman called earlier today. He said he'd be here at twelve." It was already half past. I then turned directly to Cohen, "I put your pistol in the upper draw. Where's Michael's gun? Is it the Astra [a 9mm pistol]?" Wanting to ensure that the detectives monitoring my transmitter had some idea how many weapons these people had, I continued. "You guys are dangerous with all these guns laying around." Cohen, looking for his gun, couldn't locate it. I pointed it out, saying, "In the top drawer, top drawer, top drawer. Right in there." He began to manipulate the weapon. I reminded him, "It's fully loaded, watch it."

Cohen, still fumbling with the pistol, said, "I know."

"I know you know, you loaded it." Cohen then attempted to make the weapon safe by working the action, which is precisely how one does not do that. I reached for the gun, saying, "It's loaded, yo-yo. Give it to me. Before you blow someone's head off."

Cohen asked, "Is there a round in the chamber?"

"Yeah, there's a round in the chamber."

Cohen racked back the slide. A live round was ejected as another entered the weapon's chamber. A bit flustered by my badgering, in an annoyed tone of voice he said, "Now there is."

Clearly, someone was going to get hurt if I didn't do something. I said, "Schmuck, give me the gun. You're going to hurt yourself. Let it go. Give me the gun. Let it go."

With the gun now in my hands, I cleared the piece and handed it back to Cohen. Then, turning to Fisher, I asked, "What do you got, the Astra?"

"Yeah."

"Fully loaded?"

"Yeah. But there's nothing in the chamber."

"Smart. Otherwise it can go off . At least it's not rusting to death."

"What?" he snapped back, offended by my remark.

"At least it's not rusting to death."

"Why should it be rusting?"

Of course, I didn't care about rust on the pistols or anything else. My sole goal was to inform the outside officers exactly what weapons these people were armed with. But I carried on with my bluster, "Every time I look at these damn things you guys let 'em rust."

In a defensive tone of voice, and now a bit angry, "Which one's rusted?"

Placating him, I answered, "I didn't say it's rusted, I didn't say it's rusted. Relax."

I then tried to move the subject on to the night's bombing, asking, "So what's the situation, does anyone know what the situation is?"

Hershman shrugged, "Wait for Kayman."

"Wait for Kayman. You know we got fifteen pounds of hypnole over there." Again, stating the obvious was my attempt at keeping the detectives outside informed.

"It's just hypnole," Hershman added.

"Just hypnole? Ron, you've got enough there to blow up an army."

Now that I let the detectives know what weapons and explosives were around the JDL office, I brought up the gun store in which the JDL purchased a goodly number of their firearms. "Our friend Dau-Sons is gonna have kittens, you know."

The three men gave me a quizzical look. I inquired of the trio, "Didn't Hy mention that the FBI were there?"

Taken aback by what I'd just said, Fisher asked, "Where?"

"At Dau-Sons."

He continued, "For what? For what?"

"They wanted to check on the .308's."

All at once the men began to babble among themselves. Clearly, no one had bothered to tell them of the potential legal predicament they were now in. I continued, "What'd you expect?"

Cohen, ignoring my comment, asked, "Who said that?"

"Bieber."

"How'd he know?"

"Because Dave Sommer told him. How did Dave Sommer know? Because Dave from the gun shop called him up."

Cohen immediately realized that all those guns as well as the thousands of rounds of ammunition which had been signed for with fictitious names would now come back to haunt them. The funny thing was, they could have purchased all those items legally had they used their correct names.

Cohen softly whistled, "Holy shit."

"Yeah."

Fisher added, "All the addresses are wrong and everything."

"I know, you guys fucked up all the addresses and stuff." After a brief pause I couldn't resist adding, "Crime doesn't pay."

Cohen, clearly concerned, exclaimed, "Oh, shit!"

It was then decided that the best plan of action at the moment was to go get something to eat. Cohen wanted to take his 9mm along. I argued him out of doing that. We all then stepped out for a snack at the small diner just next door.

It was well past 1 A.M. when we returned. There was no Kayman. The little band of bombers debated among themselves what to do. To Cohen, the problem was that the retaliation had to take place, if not that night then some other. Fisher agreed, but it was Hershman who raised a wrinkle. He thought that Kayman's actions suggested the man might be a law enforcement agent of some sort. It was Hershman's belief that if Kayman didn't show up that night the whole bombing plan should be abandoned. Cohen thought that, even without Kayman, he could pick up a few additional chemicals, make up some sort of device and blow the place the next night. When Kayman failed to show by 2 A.M., Hershman telephoned Bieber and told him that the three bomber hopefuls, Cohen, Fisher and himself, would be coming by to talk the situation over. Once more all I could do was go home, knowing that police officers would be remaining by the community center until daylight.

I don't recall why, but for some reason I had to return to my back-up detective my Kel transmitter that night. My instructions had been, after the completion of whatever I was doing that evening, I was to go to the west side of Manhattan, to a vacant lot alongside the East River.

It was probably near two-thirty in the morning when I finally pulled into the deserted place. Another car pulled in after me. I got out and, leaving my jacket behind and thus exposing the .45 on my hip, walked over to the detective who stepped out of the large dark unmarked police car. He was a man I had never met before, taller than me and quite a bit beefier. I so rarely had a chance to interact with other members of the department that I wanted to chat a bit with the guy. He, on the other hand, was bleary-eyed and clearly had no desire to waste time chewing the fat with this young undercover.

As I undid the transmitter from my body and prepared to hand it over to him, I made small talk, attempting to discuss where I thought this bombing plot was headed. Suddenly a worried look came over him and he said, "Uh oh." He motioned for me to turn around. In the dark shadows of what I had thought to be an empty lot was a car. It was perhaps twenty feet away. Inside sat a young couple, their eyes bulging at the sight of two large men, one who had arrived in a rickety VW beetle dressed in jeans and packing a pistol, the other in a suit. I can't imagine who they thought we were or what we were up to. I'm sure they didn't take us for the police. They were clearly terrified. My attempt at male bonding ended abruptly. The detective took my transmitter and quickly got back into his car as I got back into mine.

The next morning I called the JDL office and spoke to one of the kids who had been there the night before. According to him, Kayman had shown up a half hour after the rest of us had left. And he had had an explosive device with him.

The next day, it was a Friday, I received a call from Kayman. At this point I was ready to shoot the guy myself. The reason he gave for being late the last two nights was that he had been involved in a formal dinner with a colleague in up-state New York. Why anyone would set themselves up as the pivotal person in a bombing plot in the city, when they knew they'd be at a social event with other people seventy-five miles north of Manhattan, I was unable to comprehend.

But Kayman was indignant, "Why didn't you wait for me, I was only a half an hour late?"

"You were two and a half hours late. You said you'd be there at midnight."

"No, no," Kayman insisted. "One. I said I'd be there at one sharp." He got around to telling me he had called Hershman, who told him to relax and rest, that there'd be no attempt in the next few days. I'm sure at this point Hershman didn't trust Kayman as far he could throw him. For myself, I figured either the guy was an absolutely brilliant investigator or a bumbling idiot. And while I knew that my police superiors would never have permitted me to procure materials to make a bomb, nor help in its construction, there was the chance that if the man was a federal agent, their rules were different from the ones I had to follow.

Kayman then told me he had asked Hershman if he could "work" — con-struct his bomb — at the JDL office. Hershman told him, "You'd better not." I could just about read Hershman's thoughts during that conversation. Here was this guy who couldn't show up on time two days in a row and now he wants to build his bomb right in the JDL office.

Maybe Kayman was an agent after all. To my mind his actions were other-wise irrational. He was supposedly a professional person, a dentist, an anesthe-tist; yet, he was running around in the middle of the night carrying homemade bombs for a bunch of kids to deliver to a place, the location of which he wasn't even sure of.

Who was this guy?

CHAPTER SIXTEEN

FINALLY

It was Monday, August 24th, and I was once again up at camp JeDel. The place was buzzing with the word that the Uzi machine guns, shipped in crates marked as religious articles, had arrived by ship from Israel and were sitting at the dock in New York City, along with some 9mm ammunition.

Bieber, Cohen and Sommer all confirmed this arrival to me. The stuff was there, now, waiting to be picked up. There was even a new guy at camp, someone from Canada, who, according to our head of security, was here to train us in how to fire the new weapons.

There was only one small problem. The story wasn't true. It was all a fantasy of theirs. Bieber later claimed someone had called him a few days earlier with the information. But in fact, there were no JDL submachine guns sitting at some New York City dock, waiting for us to come and get them. The guns never had been there, nor was I able to figure out how this strange tale had spread in the first place.

Around noon, Cohen and I drove into Ellenville and walked over to the gun shop. The owner took one look at us and had kittens. He told us the FBI — they turned out to be Alcohol, Tobacco and Firearms agents — had again been to his shop asking about the various JDL members. The impression the owner had gotten from the agents was that arrests would soon be made of some of the people who had bought guns and ammunition from him. Cohen and I left the store. He had a worried look on his face. The little game that everyone was playing was about to get very real.

That evening, after I did some training with the Oz A members using one of the 9mm pistols, Cohen called Bieber, telling him of our conversation at the gun store and of the federal agents' inquiries.

At that point, the rumor about the Uzis was still very much alive. Cohen asked Bieber about the status of the submachine guns. The other man replied that he didn't know their exact whereabouts, but when he got them he'd bring them to camp. Here the guy had just been informed that federal agents were asking pointed questions about the illicit activities of various JDL members and he was going to bring a shipment of incredibly illegal machine guns to the camp. Bieber, and the JDL, were indeed lucky those guns were only someone's fantasy.

The next day Cohen and I were back at the gun store. We'd just missed the "FBI" by two hours, the owner told us. There had been more probing about the summer camp and those who were in it. The long and short of it was, he wouldn't be selling gunpowder to us any longer.

Cohen and I left the small establishment and walked back out onto the town's main street. Cohen was really concerned now, and told me he'd be getting a passport. According to him, it was JDL policy to flee to Israel rather than face a long jail term in the States.

Around one-thirty Kayman showed up, bringing his usual bag of toys. There were some chemicals in cans, assorted gun powders, thin aluminum tubes, ether — I had no idea what for — plus various other containers and objects purloined from the hospital where he worked. There were also a number of firearms in his car's trunk.

Cohen, some of the Oz A people and I, a half dozen of us all together, once again watched Kayman try to make a bomb. During one such attempt it was necessary to mix together a batch of the chemicals he'd brought. Carrying the required containers of "stuff," as well as a metal pan he used for the actual mixing, we all crammed into one of the camp's rundown single room cabins.

The place was dark and cramped, perhaps twelve by eighteen feet. A desk and some old wooden chairs further cluttered up the room. Kayman sat down by the ancient desk and poured out a quantity of his alchemist's concoction onto the freshly washed pan. I stood a bit behind him, watching him do the mixing. I chose that moment to unbutton my jeans in order to tuck in my shirt.

My timing couldn't have been worse. My fly was unzipped. With one hand I pushed my shirt below the belt line while holding up my pants with the other. As I was doing this, I began to hear a popping sound. The noise very quickly grew in strength and rapidity. Smoke started to rise from Kayman's lap. He jumped up and yelled, "Get out of here!"

The five men in front of me moved as one to the cabin's lone door, tightly shut to keep our activities hidden from the eyes of the campers. With one of my hands still needed to keep my pants up, I found myself mashed against the inward opening door. Although only moments had passed, the smoke was by then filling the cabin. With a mighty collective heave we backed up, yanked the door open and tumbled one on top of the other down the steps and onto the grass, my jeans now around my knees. Somewhere in that heap of humanity I heard Kayman's voice recalling that the chemicals he was mixing reacted violently to water. Sharp guy.

Rising to my feet, half dressed in the middle of Camp JeDel, I asked myself how come such embarrassments never seemed to happen to James Bond.

This fiasco was the last straw for Cohen. He spat out, "Screw this," and stormed off to get one of the pipes we'd so subtly purchased earlier that summer. I followed along and helped carry a drill, some chemicals, a fuse and other odds and ends to the same cabin we'd just toppled out of.

As I stood over his shoulder, he took the pipe, now capped at one end, and placed it between his legs. First he filled the large metal container with hypnole. Then, taking one of Kayman's aluminum tubes, he poured gunpowder into that, placing a length of underwater fuse inside. Cohen worked the smaller tube into the hypnole, that chemical filling the pipe to the brim. Next he picked up the heavy cast iron cap end which had been sitting on the old desk, carefully centered the drill bit in its middle, and bored a hole. Running the fuse through the freshly-made opening, he then proceeded to screw the cap onto the larger pipe. With a twisting motion he turned and turned the cast iron piece. Watching the whole scene with great interest, I began to hear a crunching sound with each turn of the cap as some of the hypnole granules escaped and were ground between the twisting threads. It was only later, when I was speaking to a member of the bomb squad, that I was told the damn thing should have detonated right there.

Cohen wrapped the now complete bomb in a canvas sack and our little group walked to the back of the camp. There, in the woods, we found a large mushroom shaped boulder, about four feet across. It had to weigh many hundreds of pounds. The device was placed snug at the base of the rock. Kayman lit the fuse.

We all ran about thirty yards away. I found cover behind a big tree. As I lay on the warm ground for what seemed like a very long time, I had visions of the damn thing malfunctioning, just as with so much else we'd tried to do in the JDL. Maybe Kayman was right after all, maybe a heavy cast iron pipe couldn't be used for what we wanted to do.

Then the ground shook. A roaring sound engulfed me and a moment later, debris began to fall from the sky. The damn thing had actually worked!

We all jumped from our hiding places. Excited, like schoolboys who had just done something very naughty and gotten away with it, we ran over to the boulder, or more accurately, the place the boulder had been. It was gone; it had simply disappeared.

I picked up some fragments of the exploded bomb as "souvenirs."

Later, when we were back at the camp proper, Cohen's girlfriend told him the explosion could be heard all the way over at the main road by the camp's gate, a good half a mile away.

The next day, back in the city, I showed up at the JDL office around six. Kayman and Bieber were there, thumbing through an arms catalog. When Kayman departed, Bieber took me aside and told me he didn't trust Kayman at all. He told me there was nothing definite he could point to, just a feeling that something was wrong with how the guy acted. The big man then laughed, saying that Kayman told him that he didn't trust me. Well, at least that made Kayman somewhat less stupid than Bieber gave him credit for being.

Bieber asked if I thought I could follow the man. I told him I didn't have any experience in such matters. He then wondered if the JDL should come up with a phony bomb plot, and see if any of them were arrested. In a more somber tone, the big man mused whether or not, because of the possibility that Kayman might be an informer, he should be killed.

I wasn't about to give him my opinion on either of those two thoughts. Shrugging my shoulders, I walked away. Fortunately, for both Bieber and Kayman, nothing ever came of the ideas.

We did have one real problem. There were a heck of a lot of firearms, legal and illegal, still at the camp. And this was the last week the campers would be there. The stuff had to be removed.

So, that Thursday, a bunch of us, including Bieber, Hershman and myself, drove up to camp. Once there, Bieber confronted the Canadian man who was supposed to teach us how to use the non-existent Uzis. Bieber asked him why he had started the rumor that the Uzis had arrived. The guy replied that it was Sommer who had told him the guns were arriving. Sommer, who was right there, got excited and said that he never did any such thing, that he had had no idea machine guns were supposed to be arriving.

Who's on first?

At that point, it once again became clear to me that I was dealing with a bunch of people who were some combination of fools and neurotics.

Cohen, Bieber and I walked into the camp armory and filled our arms with guns and ammunition, twenty-two firearms in all, leaving a dozen behind. We drove back to Queens and dropped the guns off at Bieber's. Hershman got me home shortly before 4 A.M. My wife, by then used to my odd hours, never stirred from bed.

The next Monday would be my last two-day stint at the camp. I arrived early, around seven-thirty, and found that for one of the few times that summer, Kahane was there.

Cohen and I walked into the Rabbi's office and Cohen informed Kahane of the bomb he'd constructed the week before. Kahane was delighted. He wanted to see one detonated for himself. The demonstration would have to wait until the next day, however. As we spoke, the telephone rang. Kahane's brother would arrive from Israel that evening. The two brothers were meeting in the city.

Cohen then told the Rabbi about the shotgun he had which he wanted Dave at the gun store to cut down to pistol size, a serious federal crime. Kahane was less sure of that plan. He voiced the concern that should the gun store owner have problems over JDL purchases that summer, in order to extricate himself the man might turn Cohen into the police.

On Tuesday, around 10 A.M., both Kahane and his brother returned to camp. A couple of hours after the two had settled in, the Rabbi explained to us what had transpired with the shipment of machine guns we'd all been waiting on. JDL had a contact in Israel for two hundred Karl Gustaf 9mm submachine guns. These were weapons once issued by the Egyptian government, but which had been captured during one of the many wars between the two nations. They'd since been stolen from the Israeli army and the plan was to ship these firearms into the United States. Kahane's brother, an assistant Minister of Religion in Israel, had approached the former Minister of Defense, Menachem Begin, then a member of the Israeli parliament, and sought out his assistance.

Begin refused, citing the potentially devastating negative international repercussions of such an act. What was ironic was the fact that Begin had, as a young man, been the head of the military underground group, the Urgun, and had been sought as a terrorist by the British occupying forces. Had he been apprehended then, he would have been hung.

But that was then, this was now.

According to Kahane, his brother had explained to him that the first idea, of shipping the weapons over in crates marked as containing religious articles, would not have worked. The other man was sure that customs would check the boxes and discover their contents. Kahane's brother made it clear that getting those weapons to this country required Kahane himself going to Israel to make the necessary arrangements.

Later that day, around 5 P.M., Cohen constructed a pipe bomb identical to the one he'd made the week earlier. A group of us, Kahane, Cohen, Fisher, Hershman and myself, walked to the rear of the camp. As was done the first time, the device was placed by a large rock. Fisher lit the fuse and we all ran back to what we figured was a safe distance. The explosion, which came less than a minute later, was as loud and satisfying to us neophyte bomb makers as the initial one had been.

Kahane was very happy, going so far as to suggest serrations be cut into the sides of the next bomb to make the device more effective. A few of us picked up souvenirs of shrapnel. Mine would become vouchered as evidence by the NYPD.

When I got home that evening I returned one of Kayman's several telephone calls. The conversation involved the usual grandiose plans of his for procuring quantities of weapons, ammunition and explosives for the organization. It was all becoming more than a bit tedious. What he wanted more than anything was for Bieber to get some signed, dummy FFLs to him so he could buy firearms. Kayman complained that Bieber was supposed to have called him that day, but as yet hadn't done so. I, of course, knew that Bieber had no trust in the man, so there wasn't going to be a phone call. He then asked me, in a roundabout way, when we were going to use our bomb. I told him I had no idea, which in truth I hadn't. He then said, "You know, Saturday night would be a fantastic time."

"Excuse me?"

"Saturday night in Philadelphia will be a fantastic time. Set it in time for Sunday morning."

What he was speaking of was a demonstration the JDL was to have in Philly against the Black Panther Party, an organization which had of late come out with some especially virulent anti-Semitic tracts and statements.

"But, in any event, I was thinking that if Cohen wanted to do his experiments, Saturday night, or at least Sunday morning, just before the meeting starts, what a wonderful way to start the meeting, with a bang."

"You mean the, uh, Panthers?"

"Yeah, Panthers."

I told him to suggest his idea to Bieber. At that point I really didn't know what to think of Kayman. On one hand, he had told Bieber I wasn't to be trusted. Now, the man was trying to get me involved in a bombing. It didn't make any sense.

After hanging up with Kayman I called Bieber, relaying the conversation to him.

"He's insisting he wants an FFL, right?" Bieber said.

"I know, he told me."

"I don't want to give him anything."

Then I related Kayman's suggestion for a bombing just before the Philadelphia demonstration, "He says we should start it off with a bang."

"Tell him to forget about it. Listen, I want you to be careful of this guy."

With the summer over, JDL activity began its more normal routine. Still, there were odds and ends that had to be dealt with, such as the cleaning of the firearms used during the last two months up in Ellenville.

That Sunday I picked up Cohen at his Manhattan apartment and we went over to Bieber's home to assist in the cleaning up of the organization's firearms. Still asleep when we got there was Kaufman, who had just gotten back from his visit to Israel.

While we were there Bieber told us that the JDL had gotten hold of a pipe threading machine, thereby eliminating the embarrassing need to buy the short pipes needed to make their bombs. The big man wanted to buy four-inch-diameter pipe, but Cohen argued that such a size would be too large for their bomb-making needs.

According to Cohen, Kaufman, who was trained in Israel, could now make successful explosive devices, albeit using military equipment. Bieber chimed in that the JDL would soon be getting such things. Was this simply more bravado, I wondered, as I ran a solvent-soaked patch through one of the guns' bores?

The really disturbing thing about that day's conversations was the fact that Bieber wanted to remove all the firearms from his and the Hershkovitzes home and store them in a more secure and secret location. And when I asked where that would be, Bieber wouldn't say.

Leaving the Bieber home, Cohen and I went to a local Queens restaurant. Just by chance we bumped into a couple of JDL members. The conversation turned to some recent Al Fatah airliner hijackings. The guys were upset, especially as one of the planes involved belonged to El Al. The three JDL members with me all felt that the organization would have to do something to retaliate for the Arab attacks.

Indeed, something would be done.

CHAPTER SEVENTEEN

RETALIATION

I knew there would be some retaliation for the Arab hijackings, but, for whatever reason, it was clear to me that I wasn't to be in the loop. Which meant, at that point, all I could do was ask apparently innocuous questions hoping that the bigger picture would emerge.

The talk around the JDL office was that Kahane had promised some serious action. Other than that, I wasn't able to even guess as to what would take place. Still, it was impossible for me not to sense both that something was up and that the atmosphere around me was not quite right.

The day after I had cleaned guns with Cohen at Bieber's, I went to JDL headquarters. When I got there, Bieber, Kahane and another member left for a meeting at Cohen's place. I was told by Bieber to remain in the office. What I didn't know then was that it was at that very meeting where the plan for the JDL to hijack an Arab airliner was formulated and agreed upon. It was in Cohen's apartment where it was determined which two members would do the actual hijacking: Avraham and Nancy Hershkovitz.

Those two were chosen because both had wanted to return to Israel anyway. And it would be a one-way operation, at least as far as returning to the States went. Once the hijacking took place they certainly couldn't come back to America. There were a couple of problems with the choice of those two people, however. Hershkovitz was not the greatest physical specimen to be found in the JDL and Nancy was only nineteen years old, with neither the training nor the tactical background needed to take on such a perilous and frightening mission.

On the other hand, of all those in the organization, Hershkovitz did have the mindset to take on the challenge. His background, while unusual from an American's viewpoint, was common for tens of thousands of souls after the second World War. He had been born in a concentration camp, saved from death only when his mother convinced the Nazis that her son was a Christian. After the war, what remained of the family sought out their father, only to discover that he had died at Auschwitz several days after Avraham's birth. Such a beginning in the world tends to give a person a most unique view of life.

With the decision made to have the Hershkovitzes do the hijacking, another problem was discussed. The act would certainly result in a strong response by our government. What was the organization to do with its weapons, now stored in the Hershkovitzes', as well as other members', residences?

Kahane decided — again, I wasn't told of this — it would be most prudent to rent an apartment in Brooklyn, just to keep their firearms, ammunition and bomb-making gear safe. So it was that Cohen's girlfriend, Eileen Garfinkle, took $500 dollars from Kahane and rented a place in Borough Park. Later, she and Kaufman would go to the apartment, inspect it, and when no one was around, begin bringing the JDL's weapons inside.

That next week, when I was at the office, I ran into Kaufman. He told me that all JDL weapons were to be rounded up. Bieber, also in the office, had one of the hangers-on drive me home and "turn in" the two long arms and three pistols I had stored in my home. The guns were to go to Bieber's. Beyond that I didn't have a clue as to where they'd be stored, nor was I ever told.

That Saturday, around 9 P.M., I found myself over at the Hershkovitzes'. Avraham and his wife were of course there, just lounging around. My task was to clean some of the weapons which had yet to be attended to. In my report of that meeting, I informed my police supervisors that I spotted an additional 10 twelve-gauge riot shotguns, and could now account for all twenty-five I believed the JDL had. I also mentioned a hand grenade body as well as its fuse assembly which was stored there.

I had brought along some cleaning equipment: a number of aluminum rods of different lengths and diameters, a bottle of gunpowder solvent, rags, bore patches and a few other necessary items. Laying my paraphernalia out on an open ironing board, I set about methodically cleaning the various firearms one at a time. While doing so, Nancy and Avraham sat opposite me, watching me work and chatting. By then, I was used to Avraham Hershkovitz speaking cryptically. As I worked on the guns, he casually mentioned that the police would crack down hard on the JDL after the next action. He didn't elaborate and I chose not to ask him what he was talking about. What I failed to understand at that time was that his remarks about the magnitude of the upcoming operation were his way of bragging about what he and his wife were about to do.

I had a big problem. Only, at that time, I didn't fully realize it. It seemed to me that the people in the JDL, at least the main players, had been acting strangely toward me since the end of the summer. Kaufman was downright hostile. As I sat on a table in the office, puffing on a cheap plastic-tipped cigar, he came up to me with a hammer and pantomimed striking me in the head. In turn I blew some smoke at him, but I was not amused. My sense was that these people were colder, certainly somewhat more distant to me, than before. The fact that I had been cut out of the meetings discussing the retaliation to the Arab hijacking I had found to be very unusual. But, there was nothing I could attribute this to. I certainly hadn't changed my pattern of behavior in any way.

The information stream between myself and the BOSSI detectives flowed only one way. Generally, this was a good way to run an intelligence gathering operation. There was no point in my BOSSI handlers telling me things which I should not know and which might cause me more harm than help. So it was that I was not told that someone in the JDL — a fact reported by the other undercover, Dick Eisner — had told people within the organization that they had seen me going into police headquarters.

The charge was, in fact, nonsense. It never happened. I have no idea who told this tale, whether they saw someone who looked like me going into that lower Manhattan building or what. I had early on in the investigation been admonished by the BOSSI detectives never to go near any police buildings. And I hadn't, except when there was good reason, such as when I was applying for a pistol permit as other members of the Palmach gun club were also doing.

Nonetheless, these people, paranoid at the best of times and now under increased pressure from the federal authorities due to their foolish acts involving fraudulent firearms purchases, believed I was a police officer. Once the dam of suspicion was opened there was no holding back the flood of innuendo which followed. For example, soon after I came under this cloud, I had an occasion to drive a member, Robert Reynolds, home. My VW bug had been acting up. It wouldn't idle properly, and when I dropped the guy off I popped the hood and fiddled with the carburetor for a few moments while parked in his driveway. The next day this same fellow shows up and tells everyone at the JDL office that the previous night I had hung around his place for a couple of minutes in order to get his address. In fact, I already had acquired his address, phone number and date of birth six months earlier; he had given them to me. But now he, a marginal player within the organization, had a story to tell in order to show the others what a big shot he was and build himself up in their eyes. So it was that they got to the right church by sitting in the wrong pew, but that didn't help me one bit.

As time went on it became increasingly clear that my handlers were aware of something going on, as around this time I was asked by them if I had gone into downtown police headquarters for any reason. The questions were almost accusatory, which was unlike them. This was not a good sign. BOSSI's ultimate decision, after I began reporting the increasingly hostile contacts I was receiving at the JDL, was for me to simply tough it out.

Thanks a lot.

The really confusing thing was that although I was under very intense suspicion by the inner circle of the JDL, mistrust which spread to a number of the other members as well, they continued to let me hang around even when sensitive matters or actions were being contemplated. For example, when the meeting had been held which resulted in the decision to hijack the airliner, I received a call, while in the JDL office, from Kaufman. He asked me to bring two electrical fuses to the Cohen apartment. I did that, after first jotting down the exact style and type of fuse they were. Much later I found out the guy was in fact contemplating making a bomb timing device. Why have me bring one of the components?

When Kahane heard the stories about my being a police officer, it was his idea to permit me to stick around. His theory was, at least the JDL would know who the undercover cop was. If I was tossed out, they wouldn't know who would be sent to replace me. A tactic that might be described as: an undercover in the hand is worth two in the bush. It seemed to me that their response to the situation as they believed it to be was not terribly clever.

After the Arab hijacking of the El Al jet, one of the first acts of retaliation on the part of the JDL had been to break into and ransack the New York City PLO office. Furthermore, according to what Hershkovitz told me, in Montreal, members of that chapter firebombed three Al Fatah meetings.

It was around this time that the ATF, who had become sufficiently concerned with the organization's unusual and questionable firearms purchases — they were as yet unaware of the JDL's bomb making attempts — tried to insert an agent of their own. One Monday, while I was in the office, a young man about my age walked in and joined the JDL. He gave his name as Mark Gold — not his real name. A big guy like me, his story was that he drove a cab. (I needed this, right?) He also dropped the fact that he had a couple of handguns; the same as my own two, a short barreled S&W and a .380 Walther PPK. From the moment he walked into the place, everyone in the office distrusted him. I immediately sensed he was law enforcement; too bright, too stable, too normal. But, instead of partaking in a "seduction" as was the technique of the NYPD, the ATF's approach was more akin to a "rape." Both their timing and tactics were doomed to failure. In truth, there wasn't much else they could have done, coming in as late to the game as they had.

Mark offered to drive me home. On the ride to Brooklyn, he was quite aggressive about what he knew and what he could do for the organization in the way of procuring guns and dynamite. While I sat and listened to his pitch, I sighed and figured that at least I didn't have to take the train home that night.

Sometime later in the investigation, Mark once again gave me a ride to my house. Even though it was late at night, I invited him in and gave him a cup of coffee. Mark went on about his speaking to Bieber and offering to get dynamite from a friend in construction. He also claimed he could come up with some submachine guns as well. Mark then told me Bieber had informed him that the only two law enforcement agencies that would be interested in the JDL were the FBI and the NYPD. God knows how Bieber had deduced that bit of erroneous intelligence. Mark mused that Bieber's internal security precautions were useless. He went on, saying that the FBI only used informants, which were therefore undetectable as law officers, which they were not. As for the NYPD, it was his opinion that that agency covered the tracks of their people so well that they were undetectable as belonging to the department.

At least Mark's views on this subject were accurate.

Three weeks had gone by since the PLO airliner hijacking. Tension was running high within the organization. Sunday, September 27th, found the Hershkovitzes at Kennedy Airport. Their airline tickets had been purchased using cash, for a BOAC flight to London. Both of them were armed with two concealed and loaded handguns each. In addition Nancy had a live hand grenade taped to her thigh. They were to take their flight, land in London and, once there, meet two other JDL members and give each of those two individuals a pistol.

The ill-conceived plan, concocted by the JDL as their way to retaliate for the earlier PLO hijacking, was to commandeer an Egyptian aircraft bound for Cairo and divert the plane to Israel. I have no doubt that the Israeli government had never been consulted about this mindless plot, for surely those in power there would have been appalled and would have tried to stop it. Had the Hershkovitzes succeeded it would have caused an international problem of gargantuan proportions for the governments of both Israel and the United States.

At the airport, Nancy successfully made it through security. But her husband, a gangly and awkward-appearing man, aroused the suspicion of airport authorities. It was less than three weeks since the earlier hijackings and the security personnel on duty were cautious and alert.

A BOAC security officer stationed at the check point didn't like something about Avraham's demeanor and stopped him. Nancy, who was by then in the clear, saw her husband was having a problem. She should have kept walking and found a quiet place to dump her weapons. Instead, armed with two loaded handguns and a grenade, the young woman returned to the security gate. The results were inevitable. Both of them were searched, their weapons found and they were placed under arrest.

Things were not going well for the JDL.

The day after the abortive hijacking attempt, I was at the JDL office. Bieber looked worried. He came up to me and asked, whether it was a rhetorical question or something else I cannot say, why the government would be interested in going after the JDL. He wanted to know why the authorities didn't crack down on the Minutemen instead.

To this inane series of questions I replied, "How should I know?" Had he given some thought to his own words for a moment he might have reasoned that actively trying to hijack an airliner might indeed be one way to increase the suspicions and interest of law enforcement.

Later that evening the Hershkovitz hijacking attempt was talked about by the people at the JDL office. Kahane told everyone who was in earshot, although I suspect his little speech was really for me, that he had no idea the couple would try and do such a thing. Bieber took me aside and told me that the handguns the Hershkovitzes had on them didn't belong to the organization. Of course, they just happened to have the same serial numbers as ones I had recorded from JDL-owned weapons.

On the evening news I watched as Kahane tried to explain away what had happened. Asked why the young couple was attempting to bring several loaded handguns and a hand grenade aboard an airliner, Kahane replied, "Israel needed all the guns it could get."

Really, Rabbi.

A couple of days later, I saw Eileen Garfinkle hand an Afro style wig to Cohen. Later, when I was with Cohen at his Manhattan apartment, he told me that the original plan had been to bomb someplace in retaliation for the hijackings. Now, it was up to Kahane as to what to do next.

One Tuesday evening in early October, I went down to the office. During my time there I noted that neither Kaufman, Cohen nor Garfinkle were around. It was around eleven that night when a bomb would go off at the PLO office in Manhattan, doing considerable damage. Witnesses told police that moments before the explosion a young man, carrying an attaché case, had gone into the building and had been taken to the third floor by the elevator operator.

A short time later a cleaning woman saw the same individual standing by the elevator. He seemed to be in a hurry and was quite nervous. She showed him where the stairs were and he hurried down. She described the person as being in his early twenties and, beside remembering the green military-style jacket he wore, she noted that he had a rather distinctive Afro type haircut.

That night a message was received at United Press International. A woman's voice stated, "The PLO office at 101 Park Avenue has been bombed. Please take down the following message: "'Hijack blackmail freed seven terrorists. Never again!'"

Never Again was, of course, the motto of the JDL.

CHAPTER EIGHTEEN

STRANGE BEDFELLOWS AND ANNOYING THE SOVIETS

Tension only increased within the JDL. Their actions were becoming more violent, their leadership under more legal pressure — both real and perceived.

That fall there was an incident in the Borough Park section of Brooklyn. The neighborhood, once predominantly Jewish, had undergone a change. Jews were now a minority group within the area's population. The event in question took place on a Saturday evening, during Yom Kippur services. This is a most holy day in the Jewish calendar, when people atone to God for their sins.

For some reason, a group of around fifty people, believed and reported to be Puerto Rican by those inside the synagogue but who knows for sure, attacked the worshippers within. Bricks and rocks were heaved through the windows, and when anyone attempted to leave they were pummeled by the mob outside. Even a garbage can was thrown through one of the windows, forcing the people inside to take cover under the synagogue's wooden benches.

It had been an ugly scene, the violence mindless.

Upon hearing of the attack, Kahane was infuriated. The following Monday, there was a show of force from the JDL. I, along with about seventy-five other JDLers, patrolled the neighborhood. As we marched up and down the dingy Brooklyn streets, I found myself walking alongside Dick Eisner. Although it was never deliberate or planned, he and I tended to hang out together at demonstrations. It wasn't that we were aware that we were both police officers, we most certainly were not; it was just that he and I had far more in common with each other than with anyone else in the group we'd been assigned to infiltrate.

Dick told me that the previous day he'd had a talk with Kahane. The Rabbi had told him he wanted a group of JDL members to get hold of some of the neighborhood's Puerto Ricans and beat them up until they revealed who was responsible for the assault on the synagogue. If that tactic didn't work, Dick had been told by Kahane that he wanted the neighborhood burned down.

Burn down a neighborhood where thousands lived because several dozen people, who might or might not be from that particular neighborhood, had committed an ugly act? It was pretty much the same tactic the Nazis used when dealing with the civilian populations of the countries they invaded during the Second World War. I guess Kahane figured that if burning down someone's village worked for the Nazis it must have proved to be a powerful disincentive.

It seemed to me that Kahane was becoming increasingly violent. In a speech I attended shortly afterward, he was asked by someone in the audience whether he condoned murder. His reply was, "If circumstances warrant it, it must be done."

It appeared to me that the man's thinking was becoming dark indeed.

A week or so later, there was another incident in the same general area. This time one of the members told me that two Jewish workers had been shot.

There would be another gathering of JDLers in the neighborhood. And this time at least some of the members would be armed.

Just prior to the abortive Hershkovitz hijacking attempt, most of the group's weapons had been removed from the locations which I knew about. Kahane had given Garfinkle money to rent an apartment in the Borough Park section of Brooklyn. She and Kaufman did so, and the JDL's firearms were hidden inside. The sole purpose of the place was for weapons storage. Their logic was, if one of the JDL members actually lived inside, then the place would be vulnerable to police search.

Kaufman had been sent to the apartment to pick up some pistols. In this instance, the JDL, and Kaufman, were very lucky. Not only was that man streetwise, he was very nearly paranoid. Walking up to the apartment building, he saw strange men sitting in unmarked cars outside the place. His instinct told him to keep on going.

Unbeknownst to him, three days earlier there had been a water leak coming from the JDL-rented apartment. No one was home to let the superintendent in to fix the problem. The building's owner, when the problem was explained to him, told his employee to call the police and have them accompany him inside the apartment, for protection from a claim of theft on the part of the absentee renters.

Two officers arrived from the 66th Precinct. Because the door had a lock on it for which the superintendent didn't have a key, the officers had to go in by climbing the fire escape and forcing open an outside window. Once gaining access to the apartment, the officers opened the front door for the super. To his, and their, surprise, the place was empty of any furniture. They looked around and, inside the various closets, found an arsenal of firearms and explosives.

When it was all counted up, the police removed fifty-seven long arms, sixteen handguns, over ten thousand rounds of ammunition, a hundred and ninety pounds of explosives, six pipes for making bombs, a blasting cap and underwater fuse. On top of that, beside some anti-Arab and anti-Black Panther literature, there was a list of JDL members. BOSSI was notified at once.

I only knew of the discovery of the weapons cache after reading about it in the *Daily News*. And nobody in the JDL was about to give me the straight scoop. Sheldon Davis, who now worked in the JDL office, went so far as to tell me the weapons were definitely not the JDL's.

But not everyone was on the same page. A few days after reading about the police discovery, I was at a JDL-sponsored demonstration. There, Dave Sommer told me that the dealer who had sold the organization the shotguns had called him, telling him that police had been over to his store asking questions about the weapons. "Be careful," Sommer advised me.

Another member, a teenager who spent much time in the office, took me up to the roof so we could speak privately. He let me know that the FBI — I'm sure it was agents of the ATF but I wasn't about to correct the kid — had been over to one of the member's homes and had asked numerous questions about several JDL members, myself included. That was good as far as I was concerned. In fact, I was a prime target of the ATF at that time, and indeed came very close to being picked up by that agency.

The young man couldn't understand why the police and government were taking so long to crack down on the JDL, especially after the hijacking and now the weapons cache incident. I suspected a number of those in the organization wondered the same thing. I certainly did.

Within two months the JDL suffered two serious and embarrassing setbacks: the poorly planned and executed hijacking attempt and the loss of its weapons. I can only conjecture on the confusion which must have taken hold of its leadership during this period.

Yet, even as the problems for the JDL mounted, the organization became more and more aggressive in its tactics.

It was around this time, late fall, that a dozen Jews attempted to escape the Soviet Union by hijacking a large single-engine Aeroflot aircraft and flying it to Sweden. Their plan, already known to the secret police, never had a chance of success.

They were arrested, a trial was held, and several death sentences were handed out. If the Soviets were going to make life tough for Jews in their country, Kahane would make life unpleasant for Soviet citizens in New York City.

A campaign of harassment began. Members of the Soviet Mission, whose building was located in the heart of Manhattan, were followed, on foot and by car, and tormented. Cars coming out of the Mission, easily recognized by their diplomatic plates, were trailed by organization members and, when possible, sandwiched between two JDL autos. The JDLers would then alight and run over to the Soviet's car, terrorizing the driver. People coming out of the Mission would be followed into restaurants or while shopping and subjected to the tormenting of JDL members. Russian children, arriving from school by bus, or out on a walk with their mothers, were screamed at in the vilest Russian words the JDLers could come up with.

The incidents were becoming not only a nightmare for the Soviet citizens the JDL harassment was directed at, but a serious political problem for this country as well. It came perilously close to causing a major diplomatic rift between the two superpowers. The JDL's actions were common points of discussion between the highest levels of both governments. *The New York Times* reported that the First Secretary of the Soviet Mission called it all a "campaign of outrages, provocations, vandalism and acts of hooliganism by a gang of fascist elements." Notes were passed from the Soviet Mission to the United States Mission demanding that drastic measures be taken to suppress the anti-Soviet activity. Kahane was even invited in for a talk with the United States Ambassador to the United Nations, Charles W. Yost. Yost attempted to get Kahane to agree to stop using such tactics against Soviet diplomats. Kahane, delighted by the conflict he was causing, told Yost, "If the United States really feared a threat to the *detente* which both it and the Soviets wanted so badly, that was exactly what the whole JDL plan against the Soviets was aiming at." The price for peace was absolute freedom for Soviet Jews to leave Russia.

For those in power in the Soviet Union, it was impossible to understand how the American authorities could not have a direct hand in the actions of JDL members. Freedom of speech and basic constitutional guarantees of political expression were simply concepts they could not comprehend. But Kahane not only understood the American system, he knew how to exploit it thoroughly.

One day, as I approached Third Avenue and 67th Street, during one of the many times I was to find myself at the Soviet Mission, I spied Hershman on the corner. As I walked up to him to say hello, he took me by the arm, headed me down the street, and urgently whispered in my ear, "Watch that yellow car."

At first I wasn't sure what he was talking about. The scene was typical for a JDL demonstration. A dozen or so people, placards in their hands, walked round and round on the sidewalk opposite the Mission's heavy metal gates. At the gates were half a dozen uniformed police officers standing alongside the gray wooden police barricades and chatting amongst themselves.

The one yellow car I spotted, at that moment immobilized in traffic, had two young people inside. Then, as the cars in front of it moved, I saw that the yellow car remained motionless. Once there was sufficient space in front, it quickly shot forward. Upon coming to the side of the Mission's gates, the yellow car first backed up several yards and then, with the driver yanking the steering wheel hard left, shot ahead and directly at the police guard standing outside.

Barriers flew and police officers dove for cover as the yellow car jumped the curb and came to a stop just short of the gate. As the officers were busy dealing with the car's occupants, half a dozen of the JDL demonstrators attempted to get across the barriers. None of them succeeded and several were arrested by the very shaken police officers. A couple of the JDL members were beaten by officers, both on the street and inside the station house.

A day and a half later, the JDL would make another point in their fight for the release of the Soviet Jewish prisoners. The Soviet Consulate Tourist offices, Aeroflot on one floor, Intourist on another, were bombed.

The Associated Press received a call shortly after: "Let the world know, that while Jews are on trial in Russia, the Soviet Union will be on trial. Never Again!"

The Soviet government was incensed, which is exactly what Kahane wanted. It was his desire for there to be a split between the Soviet Union and the United States. The question Kahane was trying to force was this: Was such a potentially dangerous situation worth all the trouble those damn Jews were causing? Would it not be simpler, Kahane hoped the Soviets would ask themselves, to simply let them leave the country?

A day or so after the blast, I noticed, on Kahane's desk at the JDL office, a news clipping detailing the most recent bombing. On top of the headline were the handwritten words, "I would have gladly framed this for you, but I've heard modesty is best, Eileen."

Bombing Soviet installations served a number of purposes in the eyes of Kahane. About this one he wrote, "By coincidence the JDL had scheduled a press conference the next day after the bombing to discuss the Leningrad trial of the Aeroflot hijackers, and the packed room provided a glorious opportunity to discuss the plight of those Jews, an opportunity that would certainly not have been at hand, if not for the bombing."

Explosions got attention, and it was attention that Kahane desperately needed in order to accomplish his goals. He believed that well-behaved minorities received only the most superficial notice by authorities. It was a theme he would repeat over and over in his speeches and statements. The docile, assimilated Jewish American power structure would never do anything which would embarrass themselves or their constituency. Therefore, they could safely be ignored by the government.

During the Second World War, a group of American Jewish leaders met with authorities asking that some action be taken to stop the slaughter of civilians in Germany. They were tame in their interaction with the government. It was Kahane's view that those same men, once it became clear their pleas were being shrugged off, should have created an embarrassing scene for the United States. If necessary they should have gone to jail to get their message across. He would not repeat their mistake. If Russian Jews were at risk, Soviet citizens would suffer the consequences. If innocent people had to die, that was the price to be paid.

CHAPTER NINETEEN

OLD ENEMIES, NEW FRIENDS

By December, my continued presence around the office and assorted JDL activities, without arrests being made for all the illegal things I had previously been involved in, made members less certain I was a police officer. Weapons began to come out once again for me to inspect and repair, and the talk was that I'd be the one to set up the yet-to-be-established JDL range. One short-lived experiment had the members using an informal indoor range which was nothing more than the basement of an old building. Fisher once explained to me that although the JDL was infiltrated by the police, Kahane figured they wouldn't be bothered if members only shot .22's. Whatever.

One evening in February, while I was at the main office in Manhattan, Bieber asked if I could help protect Kahane at a rally where he was to give a speech in Buffalo, New York, the next day. Trouble was anticipated from a number of protesting student groups. The next day Hershman gave me a blank JDL check, actually from one of its sub-units, Jewish Operation Youth, and off I went to La Guardia airport to meet Ralph Kaufman. Somehow it had fallen to Kaufman and me to be the unarmed protectors of the head of the JDL while he was up in cold Buffalo.

The flight was short, Kaufman and I arrived just before six. Kahane's plane didn't land until after seven, so the two of us just hung out around the small airport and waited.

By the time the Rabbi got in, several young men from the University of Buffalo had shown up to take us to the auditorium on campus where Kahane was to speak. As we all bundled into an old station wagon, I could plainly see our hosts were nervous.

The head of the group, all I remember of him is his name, Jack, told us that there was trouble on campus. Two radical organizations, the PLO and Youth Against War and Fascism, vowed not to permit the Rabbi to give his talk. I guess they had a problem with free speech as well as with the JDL. It was then that Jack suggested we'd all have to enter the auditorium's building by the back door.

Kahane bristled. "We go in the front door or we don't go in." The discussion was over. The Rabbi could be called many things, but never a coward.

Fifteen minutes later, when we pulled up to the campus, I could see why Jack was nervous. There was a solid mob of demonstrators standing outside the auditorium. They stood shoulder to shoulder in the frozen night, chanting and waving signs affixed to sticks declaring their various affiliations as well as their opinions of the JDL, which were decidedly negative.

Kahane, Kaufman and I stepped from the car. Kaufman took hold of Kahane's left arm, I took the right, and we marched straight into that milling mob. We walked briskly, eyes staring straight ahead. The great angry sea of protestors parted for us as we headed up the wide steps, through the front doors, into the auditorium. Walking down the long center isle, the three of us took the stage: Kahane at the podium, Kaufman and I on chairs to either side of him.

It took a moment for the nearly one thousand people in the audience to realize what had taken place. Then a mixture of catcalls, boos, hisses, applause and shouts of approbation arose from the standing room only crowd. Kahane looked on those before him and proceeded, for the next two hours, to give his speech.

I have often thought back to that night in Buffalo, New York. I've reflected on why I allowed myself be put in such a precarious spot, daring a mob of angry young men and women to stop us. I'm not really certain I have an answer. I remember I was afraid, although I didn't show it. I also recall, at that moment, to being resigned to whatever befell us. The only explanation I can offer is that it was my duty to do this thing. Therefore, as it had to be done, it was done.

Of course, Kahane was quite correct when he told Jack it was either the front door or nothing. And, I rather enjoyed standing up to the bullies that would have prevented us from exercising a fundamental right guaranteed by the very system they would have seen torn down.

In early spring of 1971, the Klu Klux Klan burned a number of crosses in Hightstown, New Jersey. While the Klan in that area might have consisted of only a handful of sociopaths, their actions generated fear far beyond their ability to cause mischief. Kahane decided that the JDL would respond in force. A demonstration was planned.

Those participating met at noon on a Sunday at the Shori DoJo. Bendel gave the seventy-five or so JDLers present a briefing on the day's activities. He made a point of telling everyone that it was "planned as a peaceful demonstration." Then he told us to hide our pipes, hammers and bats so the police wouldn't bother us.

As we were exiting the building, a member of the press asked, "I noticed some of the boys carrying baseball bats and hammers. What can they be used for?"

"Baseball and carpentry," Bendel replied.

The JDL members left New York City through the Lincoln Tunnel in a convoy of cars, vans and a rented truck. What they hadn't counted on was the sharing of information between New York City law enforcement and their New Jersey counterparts. Signs sprouted from several of the JDL vehicles reading, *Never Again! Save Soviet Jewry! Free Soviet Jewry!* Moreover, all the vehicles in the procession had been instructed to turn their headlights on. The characteristics that distinguished the JDL from other interstate travelers had not escaped the attention of the New Jersey constabulary. The truck had barely nosed out of the tunnel when state troopers pulled it over. In order to stay together, the remaining JDL cars and vans pulled to the side of the road as well.

The troopers informed those in the truck that it was unlawful for passengers to ride in the rear of such a vehicle. The driver was given a citation and the two-dozen or so JDL passengers tried to cram into the other caravan vehicles. Not everyone could fit and some had to make their way back to the city — hitchhiking, as nobody responded to their call for assistance at JDL headquarters.

Meanwhile, the Klansmen, out in full force, were showing their colors down in Hightstown. Well, at least three of them were. Oh, the German shepherd dog with them should probably be counted as well. Perhaps it would be more accurate to call that little group of hatemongers a Klannette.

The sign on the outside of their car read, *The hell with fighting the war over Nam. We have commies right here in our own backyard. Save our land, join the Klan.*

The police in Hightstown did not like the idea of the KKK and the JDL clashing in their rural town. The three Klanners (Kluxers?) got themselves busted for carrying leaded gloves and a tear gas pen. I don't know if the dog was taken into custody or, more likely, was permitted to drive their car back home. Of the four, the canine was clearly the brightest bulb in the chandelier.

The head Kluxer, Paul Woldanski (there's an Aryan name for you), told reporters as he was entering the police station, "There's five hundred Jews coming in and they're locking *me* up."

Clearly, Mr. Woldanski excelled in hyperbole.

At any rate, after the truck fiasco, the band of JDLers continued to their destination. Now, just outside of Hightstown, the police stopped the group. This time, when bats, chains and pipes were found among them, eight of the members were arrested.

We all finally got into the town at around two-thirty. First we drove down Main Street until coming to a small grassy park. After the tribulations of the road, I was surprised to see we had around a hundred and fifty people there.

There was some chanting of slogans. "What do we want? The Klan! How do we want them? Dead!" Also, "We are Jews, we couldn't be prouder! If you can't hear us, we'll shout a little louder!"

From the looks on area residents faces, I could tell they were thrilled we were there.

Bendel finally got up on a tree stump and made a pretty good speech, later reported in *The Trentonian*:

The Jewish community in Hightstown is afraid. They have closed their stores down. First there were Brown Shirts, then Black Shirts. They then burned books. Jews remained silent then. I speak of the criminal silence we have come here vociferously to dispel. We are not the Jews of silence. Hate groups will be snuffed out. Our motto applies to all people who have faced Klansmen and their supporters. Never again will we not fight back. Never Again!

The march through town was kind of anti-climactic. If nothing else the JDL had a sense of humor. Various signs could be seen, one which offered, "JDL Dry Cleaners — twenty-five cents a sheet." One of the marchers had on a bed sheet with a large Star of David affixed to it. A Jewish Klansman, perhaps?

I found it interesting that a number of the area Black residents joined us in our march. Many wore the JDL's "Never Again" buttons. I did overhear one older White woman say, "The Klan never did anything to me." After hearing that comment I figured her family really could have used a little more mixing of their gene pool.

We eventually made our way back to the park. There, the JDL member wearing the white sheet took it off and it was burned.

Bendel once again spoke, "They can burn crosses, they can threaten us, but they can't scare us. They're not so big without their sheets to hide behind. If they want trouble, we'll give it to them."

He thanked those in the community who had joined the march and the demonstration ended.

I made the mistake of letting Robert Reynolds ride in my car back to the city. While we're driving along, Reynolds asked me if I could buy him some black powder. This was the same guy who, only a couple of months earlier, when I checked inside the hood of my ailing VW bug after giving him a lift home, had told everyone that I'd delayed leaving his place in order to get his home address! Just the thing you'd ask of a guy you suspect to be a cop, right? I told him I wasn't running a gun store and he could go find his own.

Halfway back to the city, we all (this loose group of JDL members' cars) stopped at a gas station/rest area on the Jersey turnpike. Everyone got out of their cars and the next thing I saw was Reynolds mouthing off to some guy in an Air Force sergeant's uniform. It seems the sergeant and Reynolds had bumped into one another while walking opposite one another on the narrow pathway leading to the restaurant.

I watched as Reynolds continued to shoot his mouth off at the other man, who pulled an NYPD police shield out of his pocket. Obviously the guy was in the reserves on weekend duty. Reynolds wouldn't let up. The serviceman, with one eye on me, finally decked Reynolds. Frankly, if that idiot Reynolds wanted to get into a fight with someone, I sure wasn't going to back him up, especially not against a serviceman. And once I saw the guy's tin, forget about it. The sergeant/police officer walked away as Reynolds groggily got to his feet, saying, "I sure showed him."

Yeah.

Funny thing, though. Maybe two years later, I was out from undercover and assigned to the Police Academy for my six months of training. There was an awards ceremony going on in the auditorium and I wound up assisting with the program in some insignificant way. Who did I bump into in the academy elevator but that very officer from the Turnpike incident.

I introduced myself. The officer didn't recognize me at first. But as I related the earlier fight scene, I could see the light of remembrance coming on. He laughed, telling me the only guy around the fight who he was worried about in the group when he and Reynolds were going at it was the biggest one, who in fact had been me!

But the twists and turns of my adventures within the JDL were never more bizarre than when the organization allied itself with the alleged Colombo crime family. Before the alliance, however, there had almost been a war.

Somehow, I never did learn the details, the JDL had gotten hold of a building in Brooklyn. Named the Jewish Identity Center (JIC), the place was on New Utrecht Avenue in a mostly Italian neighborhood.

Joseph Colombo, head of his organization, had, for several weeks prior to the incident in question, attempted to set in motion a mutually beneficial relationship between the Italian American Civil Rights League (IACRL) and the JDL. In his position as alleged head of his crime family, he had been subjected to tremendous federal and local law enforcement surveillance. In order to reduce some of this pressure I presume he came up with the idea of forming an Italian civil rights group. He seemed to think he would be able to draw in large numbers of perfectly honest citizens of Italian extraction to such an organization. Thus, he reasoned, politicians, and presumably in turn the law enforcement community, would feel constrained to leave Colombo and his associates alone.

On the evening of the confrontation, a number of JDL members were having a party inside the Identity Center. They had gotten quite loud and a neighbor, an Italian fellow named Jimmy, came over and politely asked them to lower the noise. One of the JDLers, probably drunk, responded, "Go fuck yourself."

This was not wise.

Jimmy returned with eight friends, each armed with a lead pipe. One of the JDL members attempted to speak with the men as they approached the center. One blow knocked the young man down; he was then struck repeatedly with the pipes.

Others from the Identity Center came out, a general melée ensued, and a law of physics once again proved axiomatic: Those armed with the lead pipes win.

I learned most of this after arriving at the JDL office in Manhattan. I could see that our new office manager, Don, was very upset. Between the ongoing intense telephone conversations he was having, he described as best he could the situation that had just taken place.

Eventually, he got in touch with a chapter chairman of the IACRL, who, after hearing the story, told Don to go to the troubled area and tell the Italian-Americans there that in the morning someone "with respect" would be down to settle the matter.

The timing of the incident was particularly awkward because the coalition was just beginning to take shape between the JDL and the Civil Rights League. Indeed, only a few weeks earlier, Joseph Colombo had pinned a medal on Kahane. Shortly thereafter, both leaders had agreed to demonstrate together in support of each other's causes.

Don and I drove over to the Identity Center, where fifty JDL members were milling around. It was obvious that someone had made telephone calls because there were more people present than had been at the original incident. Among those I spotted were some of the JDL's "heavy hitters," and from what I saw and heard, they wanted a fight.

This was not good. During the confusion, I sneaked out of the building and found a street pay telephone. It was a risky thing to do, but the possibility for there to be bloodshed was just too great. I put in a call to the on-duty BOSSI detective. I suspect he then phoned the situation in to 911.

Soon, a number of patrol cars rolled onto the scene. One of the officers tried to enter the Identity Center and was blocked by a JDL member who told him he couldn't come in without a warrant. The member, using foul language and getting in the officer's face, added some insults along with his insistence that the officer observe the JDL members' constitutionally guaranteed rights.

The police did not come into the building but did ticket Fisher's car parked next to a fire hydrant. Fisher objected and he and the officer went round and round a bit. Then Don jumped into the verbal fray, telling the officer to "Fuck yourself. If we have any more problems here, we're going to burn this neighborhood down." The police on the scene managed to remain calm, a lot calmer than the screwball JDL members around them. No arrests were made.

That should have been the end of a stupid, albeit violent, neighborhood dispute. But once Kahane heard of the fracas, he was livid. The man wanted blood.

When I spoke to Hershman some days later, I was told that Kahane was set on the JDL retaliating against Jimmy. According to Hershman, the Rabbi wanted the man's store windows broken, his store burned down, and Jimmy "beaten to death."

I reminded Hershman that such an action might cause a strain between the Italian American Civil Rights League and the JDL. I also pointed out that the members of the IACRL have likely also discovered fire. Burning down one of their places would most probably have resulted in the burning down of the Identity Center. At least, for starters. Hershman assured me he had mentioned those very same possibilities to Kahane, but the man had been unmoved.

A few days later, when driving back from a demonstration in Albany, New York, the matter was again discussed. Kahane's feelings on the subject had not changed. Both Cohen and I appealed to his common sense. Such an action on the part of the JDL would cause a major rift between the local Italian community and the organization. People would likely get seriously hurt.

Kahane didn't care. As far as he was concerned, it was a matter of image. The JDL could never be seen to lose. From now on, there would be several loaded twelve-gauge shotguns kept at the Jewish Identity Center at all times.

He told Cohen and me to go out and buy them. He wanted a total of twenty such weapons purchased.

Nor had the Rabbi forgotten Jimmy. Kahane said he wanted around two dozen members available for the assault on the man and his store. The Rabbi figured the best time to do the job would be the very next week. Kahane would not bow to reason on the matter.

I was not happy about this situation. Little thought had gone into the repercussions of such a confrontation, not to mention the real possibility of miscalculation, by both sides, which was possible during the coming battle and which could lead to someone getting killed. A day later, I worked out a plausible excuse for not buying the shotguns that Kahane desired. Basically, I waited until late in the afternoon to call the gun store we would be going to. By that time it was only an hour before closing, and the store was up in Yonkers, north of the Bronx. I dialed up the office and spoke with Bendel, telling him it was now too late to get the guns that day.

When I showed up at the JDL office around 6 P.M., I found Cohen there. We discussed the still imminent assault on Jimmy. Cohen had told one of the JDL regulars to keep an eye on the guy and generally check out the area where Jimmy hung out. We'd hit him on Wednesday of that week.

A few hours later, Cohen and I wound up at Bieber's house. Once again we spoke of dealing with Jimmy. It was Cohen's opinion that the man should suffer some permanent damage, such as a broken arm. Bieber chimed in that after the guy is beaten to a pulp he should be told that if there was any retaliation his store would be blown up.

Bieber told Cohen to get six big JDL members together for the attack.

The Wednesday date came and went after it was decided by Bieber that Thursday would be better. Then Bieber called off the attack, deciding that attacking Jimmy in Borough Park where he lived and worked would be a bad idea. Kahane had heard about this and declared that that was exactly where the assault would take place.

It was then set for the next day. Five of us were assigned to do the job. Cohen had to leave that day for Washington, D.C. But before going, he demonstrated to me exactly how Jimmy's arm should be broken. We'd also have a twelve-gauge shotgun with us, loaded with buckshot.

We drove out to the Identity Center in Brooklyn in two cars. I drove along with Bieber and another man. The five of us lay in wait for Jimmy to appear. While we sat in the car, waiting, Bieber let it be known that if we couldn't reach Jimmy then at least we could deal with his family. Great.

Jimmy showed twice; both times, fortunately, with buddies. The attack was put off.

I was none too pleased about the entire situation. Understand, I have no qualms about self-defense. Indeed, I feel strongly that not to defend oneself is irresponsible and ultimately counterproductive. But to coldly attack another person just isn't my style. And that talk about the guy's family sickened me. Then there was the shotgun. Bringing that along was like taking a lit sparkler into a dynamite factory.

As with many of the organization's plans, this one too was delayed several more times. But, as it happened, during one of the demonstrations, Joe Colombo had a chance to speak with the office manager of the JDL. Colombo assured him that Jimmy had been spoken to and there would be no more trouble with him or his friends. The injured JDL members' hospital bills would be, and in fact were, paid. The JDL even got free use of cars from Jimmy instead of having to pay for rentals.

Peace at last, in Brooklyn.

CHAPTER TWENTY

OUT OF THE KITCHEN AND INTO THE FIRE

From the fall of 1970 until my part in the investigation ended, I suspect there was much confusion in the organization as to exactly who I was and what I was doing there. They certainly had no hard proof that I was a police officer, only that wild, and untrue, story about me going into police headquarters. On the other hand, I have to believe that once the seeds of doubt had been planted, every action I'd ever taken with the JDL was put under a paranoid microscope of inspection.

But they couldn't be certain. And the longer I hung around and participated in their activities, the weaker their suspicions became. Otherwise, why would Kahane have asked me to go along when purchasing shotguns for the organization, or why would Cohen first ask my advice about procuring a sniper rifle, then tell me where and when he finally bought it? Why would Bendel bring an unregistered handgun to my home for me to repair, and why would they once again store some of their firearms, two dozen surplus military rifles, at my residence?

To further complicate matters, the investigation was not going smoothly for BOSSI with their other operative within the JDL. Dick Eisner had caught a bad break.

Dick was working his way pretty deeply into the JDL even as I was struggling to stay afloat in the sea of suspicion I found myself in. A quiet, unassuming kind of a guy, his biggest problem was that he didn't act nuts, as did most of the other young active members. He used good judgment, made rational decisions and didn't fly off the handle at the first hint of confrontation or trouble.

During this juncture in the investigation, a number of bombs had gone off in the city, damaging or destroying assorted Soviet and PLO locations. All the explosions were attributed to the JDL. Demands were being placed on BOSSI to get some answers. I began to feel some of that pressure myself. But demanding an undercover to perform is analogous to building a huge fire to more quickly boil a pot of water; all you can do is stoke the fire hotter and hotter still, with dangerous consequences.

One bombing took place a few hours after I had left the office. There was no way I could have been involved with it; I wasn't part of the inner circle at that point. But that didn't stop one of the BOSSI detectives from chewing me out the next day. He told me that I should have hung around the JDL office longer. Brilliant idea, I thought. Maybe I should have told the JDL bombers, "Hey, guys, next time, before you blow something up, let me go along, okay?"

So, hedging their bets, the day after that bombing some people over at BOSSI decided they'd wire up Dick Eisner with a mini transmitter, of the type I'd used earlier, and have him hang around the JDL office. Dick did as he was told. While he was sitting at Garfinkle's desk in the JDL office, she came over to get a pair of scissors. Dick had his back to her. As she leaned over to open the drawer she spotted his body wire microphone tapped to his chest.

She left and ran over to Jake Weisel, telling him what she had just seen. Dick realized something was wrong and made it to the bathroom where he ditched the wire. He was smart enough to leave a single piece of tape on his chest for "plausible deny-ability" should any of the JDL members confront him about the matter.

I'd been wired maybe three times by various detectives from Intelligence. Some of the detectives were better at it than others; some of the wiring jobs done on me had left something to be desired. Once, I had one of the microphones fall from my chest and sit half the night by my belly button because the detective who put it on me hadn't used enough tape!

Dick's wire should never have been so easily spotted. The officer now had a problem and he knew it. Naturally, Garfinkle told Kahane about the incident and later in the evening the Rabbi called Dick in and asked him about what had happened. Dick toughed it out as best he could, showing Kahane that there was only a little piece of tape there and no microphone. Kahane really didn't know what to believe. First Rosenthal, his firearms expert, comes under suspicion; now, the cool-headed and highly respected Eisner.

Dick was permitted to continue to hang around the office, but he was never again trusted by the inner members of the organization. The investigation had been rushed and whoever rushed it blew their second undercover in the process.

The bombs which the JDL were setting off within the city, and elsewhere, continued to create a serious rift between the United States government and the Soviet Union. Those explosions, the initial ones had been spaced over a six-month period, plus the harassment of Soviet diplomats, countless demonstrations in front of Soviet and various Arab facilities, and vandalism to these same locations and others, sent the vast law enforcement machinery available to the federal government down upon the JDL. This was, of course, in addition to the increased interest the now embarrassed New York City Police Department had taken in the group.

The pressure on me continued: Because of this, I found myself spending more and more time hanging out at the various JDL offices. I certainly didn't want to appear to be a slacker in the eyes of my superiors at BOSSI should a bomb go off without my having at least been around the perpetrators.

One Monday evening, I was at the JIC when I sensed something was going to happen. After a while at the undercover game, you learn that who you don't see around you can be as significant as who is right there. Bieber was there. And, from time to time I would spot Bendel in the place. He'd go up to Kahane, whisper something in the Rabbi's ear, and leave, only to return later and repeat the performance. But, neither Cohen nor Garfinkle were to be seen. Instinct told me something was up. There had been a bomb detonated at Communist Party Headquarters in Manhattan only a couple of weeks earlier. Bombs were definitely on my mind at that moment.

I badly wanted to know the whereabouts of Cohen. If something was about to go bang, I figured he'd be around it. After giving an impromptu lecture on firearms to the assembled audience, I was acting as filler while Kahane stepped away for a half hour or so. I went up to Bieber and concocted a plausible lie. I told him I had to see Cohen about the rifle range the Rabbi was so anxious to set up.

Bieber told me he didn't know where Cohen was, so he walked over to Kahane in the crowded room. Although I was perhaps fifteen feet away from the two men there were so many people milling around it wouldn't have been obvious to anyone that I had just been speaking to Bieber.

I watched as Bieber asked Kahane where Cohen was. I'm sure he didn't know that the reason Bieber wanted that information was because I'd just asked him. Nevertheless, Kahane's eyes turned to me, and I saw real apprehension in them as he answered, "Eileen's," then quickly walked away.

Bieber came back to me and repeated the information. Since I didn't have a clue where Eileen lived, and told Bieber so, he said he'd take me there.

Top shelf internal security all the way.

Just before midnight I followed Bieber's car to the street-level, Borough Park, Brooklyn apartment. I stayed a few steps behind Bieber as we walked around to the rear of the private home. Bieber knocked on the door, which

Hershkovitz, just out on bail from prison and awaiting sentencing for his earlier attempted airplane hijacking, opened.

Seeing me, the man blocked our way. It was near midnight, so I figured his wife might not have all her clothes on. Then, a moment later, Nancy came to the door in her bathrobe.

Bieber asked, "Where's Stuie?"

"He and Eileen went to get pizza," came the reply.

"Well, we'll wait," Bieber said as we walked inside.

The place was small and narrow. I stood in the tiny kitchen and saw that a long hallway led to the bedroom. "Sit in the kitchen," Hershkovitz said, indicating a chair.

I took a seat, knowing that I was really pushing my luck on this bit. If it hadn't been for Bieber's foolishness taking me here, this very pushy attempt at finding out what was going down would have been a disaster. But Bieber was completely insensitive to the tension in the air. He asked Hershkovitz, "Who's back there?" motioning to the far room.

"Bendel," Hershkovitz answered.

So I sat at a small wooden table, playing with a newly acquired puppy named Ralph. Then Nancy sat down with me, and Hershkovitz produced a bottle of children's bubble-making liquid.

The life of a secret agent was truly one of glamour, I mused, as we took turns blowing bubbles. While fooling around with the others in the kitchen, I noticed a great deal of activity in the rear room. I caught glimpses of Bendel scurrying about, tidying things up. In my previous experiences with him he was not all that fastidious.

After about ten minutes, Bendel came into the kitchen and, now a casual and attentive host, asked why we were all sitting in such a small room? The group got up and stepped to the rear of the house into the bedroom that doubled as a living room.

I noticed that although it was a larger area, a table and several pieces of furniture had been crowded into it. Bendel took a seat on a couch. At his feet was a military-style green canvas rucksack. From his body language, it was clear he didn't want anyone near that bag. I had no doubt a newly made bomb was inside.

On the floor, and on the nearby table, I saw little scraps of wire, some with red electrical tape attached. I wanted a piece of that wire.

So, with Bendel on the couch, Bieber reading an article about the JDL in *New York Magazine* and the Hershkovitzes puttering around the room, I decided to make a try at snagging a piece.

I began by asking about some porno magazines Cohen had told me he had around. When no one responded, I said, "Fuck you guys, if you're not going to give me the dirty magazine, I'm going to steal a cigar."

In the corner, by the end of the table, lay a pack of cheap cigars. I had to squeeze between the table and the wall to get to them. While doing so, I lay my open hands on the table and imbedded the wire in my palm. Picking up the cigars I asked, "Anyone got a match?" Using the hand with the wire embedded in it, I checked my pockets in what appeared to be a fruitless search for a light. The wire loosened and fell safely inside. Looking around the place I finally discovered a match, lit the cigar and began to relax.

A few minutes later Cohen and Garfinkle got back. As soon as she came inside the room, Garfinkle began to clean up all the remaining wire. Cohen and Bendel began to discuss where to keep "it" for the night. Cohen didn't want "it" kept at Garfinkle's place. Bendel suggested that Bieber take "it." Finally, Cohen said, "Let's not discuss it here," and Bieber and Bendel stepped outside, with Bendel taking "it" with him.

Cohen and I remained behind, where we discussed the never-to-be-built range and firearms instruction for the members.

I left the place at twelve-thirty. When I got home I called my contact and told him what I believed I had seen. I tried to get the point across that in the very near future a bomb was going to be detonated in the city. The detective didn't seem overly impressed with my thoughts on the matter and told me to report the information during my morning debriefing.

Forty-eight hours later a bomb blew up at the Soviet trading organization, Amtorg, in New York City. Four JDL members were involved in the bombing: Cohen, Garfinkle, Jake Weisel, and Sheldon Seigel (Seigel was the same man who would, only a few months later, build the incendiary device placed in the office of Sol Hurok). They would go to the building just before 6 P.M., armed with two leather briefcases, each containing a bomb. One was placed on the nineteenth-floor stairwell, the other on the floor above.

The day prior to the bombing, I had spoken to Weisel as we drove away from a JDL demonstration. At that time, he had told me he didn't like to be around Cohen and Bendel when they were making bombs; if two wrong wires touched, the thing would go off.

On the day of the Amtorg bombing, Kahane, fresh from an appearance in court for one of the many minor infractions he incurred while conducting demonstrations in the city, took a seat in his office. He asked for a radio. There was a tone of impatience in his voice. Although no one in the office knew why it was such a big deal, one was found.

Shortly after 5 P.M., a call was received at the offices of the Associated Press and United Press International. The same message was read in each:

There have been several time bombs placed in the office of Amtorg, at the Soviet freight office at 355 Lexington Avenue. They will go off in less than fifteen minutes. Free all Soviet Jewish prisoners. Let my people go. Never Again!

The building's engineer was also called. The message relayed to him was simple. "Evacuate the building. The nineteenth floor is to be bombed." The caller identified himself as being from the Jewish Defense League.

At 5:37 P.M., the first explosion went off.

Kahane, still in his office, listened to the news report of the incident. When the announcer told his audience that there had been one bomb, Kahane smiled and held up a hand with two fingers raised. He knew there were two bombs. He then closed the door to his office.

Police personnel responded to the scene and found the second device. Before it blew, a member of the bomb squad opened the satchel and snipped one of the wires.

The timing of the Amtorg bombing was not good for Hershkovitz. The next day, he was in federal court to be sentenced for his attempted hijacking of the airliner. The federal judge gave him the maximum sentence, five years in prison.

CHAPTER TWENTY-ONE

NOT WITH A BANG BUT A WHIMPER...

Life does not well mimic the neat and tidy world of fiction and fantasy. It was May of 1971. My last few weeks as an undercover officer inside the JDL held little in the way of excitement. No suspenseful music filled the air as I headed for some dramatic denouement with the bad guys. What did happen was far more prosaic; I continued to go about my business of attending meetings, speaking to people and making out my police reports.

I do not know, nor have I ever found out, precisely why the hierarchy of the NYPD, and presumably the ATF, decided it was time to arrest Kahane and the others within the JDL who had committed the various violations of law which I had observed, and which those two police agencies had independent knowledge of. I suspect the Soviets were livid over the matter of the April 22nd bombing of Amtorg and that probably had a lot to do with it. Now, with the arrests of the JDL members, the government could claim it was "doing something."

Shortly before the arrests, I had gone before a federal grand jury to give my testimony. This, and other evidence I am sure, resulted in the indictment of a number of JDL members on assorted weapons and bomb-making violations. At the time, I was unaware that the ATF had an informant within the JDL. This was the person (I never actually met the man) who had purchased many illegal firearms across state lines, the same weapons whose serial numbers I had so dutifully reported to my BOSSI supervisors.

A day or so before the arrests were to be made, and with no other prior warning or indication, I was called by one of the BOSSI detectives. He told me what was about to happen and instructed me to meet him down by the old Police Academy building the next day. It was in this building that I had last held my shield. He added that from then on I was to make sure to carry a gun.

The news came as a relief. It wasn't that I hadn't enjoyed my work — an eclectic mixture of excitement, boredom, fear, uncertainty and youthful bravado

— but what I had really wanted all along was to be a *police officer*. And, with the ending of this investigation, I figured I would finally have that opportunity.

When I arrived downtown, I saw the detective waiting on the street just outside the front entrance to the old building. He handed me my police shield. Looking down at the small silver piece of metal, which I had first held nearly two years earlier, that initial feeling of pride, of *being* a New York City police officer, came back to me. The two of us then headed over to headquarters to have my identity card made. After that, the instructions he gave me were clear: leave my residence in Brooklyn and stay with my parents in New Jersey until things calmed down.

My wife and I had been living on the first floor of a one-bedroom apartment located on a quiet street just north of Sheepshead Bay. The area was pleasant and the rent low. We really didn't want to give the place up, especially as we were saving to build a home. So I opted to go to my landlord, explain the situation to her, and tell her we'd be leaving for a while. (It turned out we'd be gone for about four months). When I sat her down to inform her that I was in fact a police officer, and not a college student driving a taxi, the news didn't come as much of a surprise. The woman told me she had figured I had been up to something, she just hadn't been sure what. I guess it came as a relief that I was a law officer and not a drug dealer.

I was not present at the ensuing arrests. Much of the following information comes from newspaper articles at the time as well as *The Zionist Hooligans*, a remarkably thorough dissertation on the JDL by Sholomo Russ, a doctoral student from the City University of New York who interviewed me and others involved.

On May 12th, a task force of NYPD officers and ATF agents swooped down upon JDL headquarters, as well as other locations around the city. They took into custody eleven of the thirteen members of the organization who had been indicted and who they could find.

Ten agents rushed into the office. Garfinkle, seeing the armed men were fair-haired and had blue eyes, thought they were Nazis retaliating for a recent JDL attack. She figured this was the end. It took a few minutes for one of the agents to identify himself, at which point Garfinkle realized with some relief that she wasn't going to be shot, only arrested.

Sheldon Davis, a gun muzzle pressed to his chest, asked which agency the officer represented. When told the Treasury Department — of which the ATF is a branch — the young man was confused, wondering if he had in fact forgotten to pay his taxes.

Kahane was at the JDL's attorney's office in Manhattan, along with Bieber and another indicted member. Agents stopped the three men as they were leaving. When the law officers asked Bieber his name, he gave them a phony one. Since it wasn't on the agents' list of those to be arrested, he was let go. Bieber wasted no time. He rushed home and rid his house of the various items of illegal material he had stashed there. After ditching the stuff, he returned to his residence. ATF agents were waiting for him.

Cohen had driven up to JDL headquarters as the arrests were being made. Warned off by one of the members, he and another JDLer went to Kennedy Airport and, using false names, took a hotel room for the night. Although he considered fleeing to Canada and from there on to Israel, Cohen, accompanied by an attorney, turned himself in when he found out those arrested had been released on bail.

Kahane, who by that time was sitting in the Federal House of Detention in lower Manhattan, decided he needed a good lawyer. He called upon Barry Slotnick, who also happened to be the attorney for alleged organized crime boss Joseph Colombo.[1] In fact, the lawyer's jailhouse meeting with the Rabbi made him late for an appointment with Colombo. Over dinner Slotnick told Colombo of the predicament Kahane was in. The Rabbi had insisted that all the other JDL members would have to be bailed out first, before he would leave jail. Colombo, impressed with Kahane's ethics, put up the bail money for the entire group of eleven. Two members had escaped apprehension; both Ralph Kaufman and Nancy Hershkovitz had fled to Israel.

Later, when he was finally released from detention, Kahane was asked by a reporter, "What's your philosophy behind this alliance?" referring to Colombo's arranging the substantial bail required to set the JDL members free.

Kahane replied, "I'm not a philosopher. This morning I am a defendant." More than glib, Kahane was a practical man. Shunned by the major Jewish organizations, he took the only help available. On the morning of May 15th, *The New York Times*, not a friend of the JDL's by any means, commented, "In his worry about his own future, it seems not to bother Rabbi Kahane that by making such an unsavory alliance he has only provided additional reason for public revulsion against his already discredited organization of strong-arm extremists."

It was only a month later that Joseph Colombo, with his attorney, Barry Slotnick, only a few feet away and while attending an Italian Unity Day event in the vicinity of Central Park, was shot by a gunman. The JDL's relationship with the IACRL began to crumble after that.

The federal charges facing the JDL members were serious: illegally purchasing firearms and detonating explosives without a proper federal permit or the payment of required taxes.

The case against them was a strong one. For the weapons violations, the government had the potential testimony of the ATF informant who had actually procured the firearms, as well as his interaction with those members of the JDL involved in the crime. As to the explosives charges, I would have made a most credible witness for the government's case. At the very start of the proceedings, a troubling issue was raised by Slotnick.[2] He asked, had there been any electronic surveillance done on the defendants that the defense should be made aware of?[3]

It was a straightforward question that elicited a circumspect response from the Assistant United States Attorney as well as the lawyer who was representing the Department of Justice. Well, perhaps some conversations had been overheard, but if so they were under the auspices of national security. And, anyway, none of the evidence obtained for this prosecution arose out of any wiretap material.

The defense attorneys were not impressed by the government's assurances. As it happened, the Nixon administration was then embroiled in a legal dispute, in a number of States, over this kind of national-security-authorized — but otherwise warrantless — electronic surveillance. And the government had been losing their argument in the courts over the matter with depressing regularity. Constitutional protections afforded citizens are not casually overlooked by the higher courts.

A week after the initial meeting in which the issue had been raised, the prosecution filed papers which stated that, yes, in fact the JDL office had been taped and a number of the defendants' conversations had been recorded. Furthermore, this wiretapping, done for reasons of national security, had been undertaken without benefit of court authorization or warrant.

The logs resulting from this surveillance, which had been turned over to the presiding judge, were several hundred pages long. After spending some time going through the document, Judge Weinstein ruled that the defendants must have access to the material in order to mount a meaningful defense. His logic was simple. If the government had come up with evidence due to information gleaned from an extralegal wiretap, the defense had a right to be made aware of this, examine the logs and/or tape, and make its claims accordingly.

The prosecution demurred, claiming that they did not have the authority to release such documents to the defendants without the authorization of either John Mitchell, the United States Attorney General, or President Nixon.

The issue at hand was a conflict between presidential power and the judiciary. The judge allowed the government two weeks to decide how they wished to handle the matter. It was clear to the defense that should the government refuse to release the wiretap evidence, the case would have to be dismissed, as it would be impossible for the defendants to mount a viable defense without having access to such material.

In an unprecedented move, the government ultimately authorized the release of the wiretap logs to the defense. Now it was up to the attorneys for the JDL members to try to find some connection between what was very likely an illegal wiretap and their clients' involvement in the case. Any material, even of the most remote nature, which could be connected to that electronic surveillance tap, would not be admissible in court.

The documents which were then released to the JDL attorneys were only summaries of the conversations recorded by the FBI. When asked for the original tapes, the defense was told that they had been destroyed — a direct violation of federal wiretap law which requires such material to be held for ten years. This put the prosecution in a terrible bind. How could it be shown that the evidence obtained against the defendants was not tainted by this wiretap, if only a synopsis of the conversations had been noted and the tapes were now gone?

Although the ATF and NYPD had made a solid case against the JDL members using an informant, an undercover officer, as well as long, hard, lawful and diligent investigative procedures, the FBI, unbeknownst to the two other law enforcement agencies, had been running what amounted to an illegal wiretap. The tap had continued even after the arrests of May 12th, and had included conversations between JDL members and their attorneys. The presiding judge was not amused.

A tug of war began. On one end of the rope were the defendants (with the exception of Kayman, who appeared ready to make a deal with the government). The other end was in the hands of a complex intertwining of governmental interests: the Departments of State, Treasury, Justice and the Office of the President. At that point in the proceedings, the case could have gone either way. The defense was having trouble connecting the evidence obtained against them with the judicially unauthorized wiretap. The government, depending on how the judge ruled, might well lose the contest by default, having destroyed the tapes which had done them no good in the first place.

The trial would have been a long one for both sides. So, between the various parties involved, a deal was worked out. Just three of the JDL members would plead guilty; Kahane, Bieber and Cohen. Charges would be dropped on all the others. The attorneys felt confident that the sentences handed down for the three would be some sort of probation, at least for the latter two defendants. As for Kahane, there was no way for the defense to tell.

When Kahane stood before Judge Weinstein, he pled guilty to detonating a bomb up at the JDL summer camp. In Kahane's words, according to Shlomo Russ, the bomb was "to graphically illustrate to youngsters of the camp the type of bomb described in pamphlets." The Rabbi claimed he had no idea it was a crime to explode such a device on private property.

The man lied to the judge. The fact was, the bombs exploded at camp were conducted well away from the prying eyes of the campers. They were constructed as a test for eventual use against those the JDL believed to be their enemies. Upon the detonation of the second device, Kahane's suggestion to serrate the outer portion of the pipe to make it more effective, tells far more about his intentions then the concocted story he presented to the judge.

The government told the defense that it was willing to go along with the proposed disposition as long as all of the JDL's guns and explosives were turned over to authorities. This was agreed upon by the defense.

On July 12th, as reported by the *Daily News*, the first batch of explosives released by the JDL was 197 sticks of Trojan brand dynamite — the same manufacturer as that used in the Amtorg bombing and which had been found in an unexploded bomb at the Soviet Mission at Glen Cove in Nassau County. Some JDL members had placed the explosives in the bushes alongside the Palisades Parkway, just over the George Washington Bridge in New Jersey. Although Slotnick had called one of the Assistant United States Attorneys to tell him that he "had had a dream" where the dynamite was to be found, a Parkway worker, mowing grass, stumbled upon the cache first. The amount of explosive was too great for even the NYPD's Emergency Service Unit to handle. The Army had to be called in in order to haul the lethal stash away to Fort Dix. In the interim the Palisades Parkway, a major metropolitan commuter route, had to be closed to traffic for hours.[4]

Distressed by the thoughtless manner in which the JDL was complying with their agreement, the Assistant US Attorney called Slotnick and told him that the next time he had a dream where such stuff would be discovered, the man should imagine it to be in a vacant lot.

The admonition had no effect. The next day Slotnick had another "dream." This time the material was to be found in a locker at the heavily traveled East Side Airlines Terminal. Sure enough, when the locker was opened there were over seventeen pounds of smokeless powder, five pounds of blasting powder and six blasting caps and fuse.

Kahane denied any knowledge of the finds. To the press, he claimed, "The JDL will not be turning in any illegal weapons because we have none."

Kahane was not intimidated by the thought of how his words might affect his sentence. Just prior to agreeing to plead guilty he had publicly stated, "I am in favor of any violence if it is necessary."

Before Judge Weinstein, on the day Kahane was sentenced, Slotnick referred to the activities at Camp JeDel as having taken place for the educational benefit of the campers. He spoke about Molotov cocktails having been made and thrown for the campers' edification as to the dangers of such things. As for the bombs, it was an idea Cohen had come up with after seeing the design in a pamphlet "put out by another group," an allusion to the Black Panther Party. These words were so much fantasy.[5]

The judge gave Kahane a chance to speak. He was a brilliant speaker, and even though he was facing a possible prison sentence, he made his position clear to Judge Weinstein. While he might be incarcerated in this life for his beliefs and actions, it was how God would judge him that was his real concern. And, when the souls of persecuted Jews would ask, "Where were you when we were in trouble?" he would be able to say that he was there for them and he did what he could.

Kahane ended his speech to the court by saying, "I have tried to do what I can and whether I go to prison or I do not, I am going to continue doing what I have to do and I only hope that the members of the Jewish Defense League and all Jews, no matter what happens this morning, will do what they have to do. Thank you."

Although there had been no trial, Judge Weinstein was well aware of the validity of the evidence against Kahane and the others in the organization. In *The Zionist Hooligans*, Shlomo Russ recounts that Judge Weinstein looked at Kahane and began,

There is no direct evidence that the 197 sticks of Trojan brand dynamite found on July 11, 1971 at the Palisades Interstate Parkway was under the control of the defendant Kahane, but there is good reason to believe that this is the case. Trojan brand dynamite was found on June 22, 1971 by the Nassau County Police at the Russian Mission to the United Nations estate at Glen Cove, Long Island and also at the Manhattan office of the Russian import firm known as Amtorg, bombed at the height of business hours...

The judge went on about the dangers the acts of the JDL presented to the general public, then discussed the public's perception, encouraged by JDL supporters, that the charges were technical in nature and were nothing more than a persecution, aimed at silencing some too-vocal Jews.

A number of the letters (received by the court) evince some misapprehension about the nature of the charges. We do not have here merely a technical failure to pay a tax on the making of a demonstration explosive device or merely one instance of detonating a demonstration bomb on private property to teach children what violence is like . . . Rather, what we have here are conspiracies to illegally obtain many guns and to illegally transport them across state lines; we have here conspiracies to illegally obtain many sticks of dynamite and great quantities of gunpowder and other explosives and to store much of this material in crowded areas . . . and then, presumably to use them.

There are some who accuse the government of persecuting these defendants by prosecuting them on technicalities. Nothing could be further from the truth. The prosecution was properly concerned with protecting many innocent persons . . . from the terrible tragedies that would have resulted had any of these explosives been set off accidentally or purposefully.

While these three defendants may believe themselves to be in a superior moral position, so far as the law is concerned when they use guns and bombs illegally they are not readily distinguishable from the Weathermen or Black Panthers on the left or the Klu Klux Klan on the right. Those groups too, use terror to encourage a way of life their members, in good faith no doubt, think needs to be encouraged and protected.

... Their plans were thwarted by a combination of good police work and chance discovery of caches of munitions. Had they used these weapons, their plea to one indictment would not have been accepted and upon conviction they would have gone to prison for many years. The fact that they showed contrition by admitting guilt, turning in all weapons and acknowledging wrong before anyone was injured must count heavily in their favor... The public will not be safer, the Court is convinced, if any of these three defendants are in jail.

The three defendants were then sentenced. Cohen, a juvenile at the time of his crimes, to three years' probation and a five hundred dollar fine; Bieber to three years' imprisonment and a $2,500 dollar fine; Kahane to five years' imprisonment and a $5,000 dollar fine. The judge then suspended the jail sentences of the two adults.

Judge Weinstein added one provision to the defendants' probation: that they may have nothing to do, directly or indirectly, with guns, bombs, dynamite, gunpowder, fuses, Molotov cocktails, clubs or other weapons.

Outside the courthouse, Kahane's supporters waited. When he emerged he was hoisted on their shoulders while those around him danced and sang. Kahane's face beamed with delight.

It very soon became clear that the leniency shown to him by the judge had not impressed Kahane. The crowd moved across the street from the courthouse where he gave an impromptu speech, "I want you to know that I can't talk about guns. But I want you all to have this," he then raised his hand, forming the symbol of the gun — a raised thumb and forefinger — to the delight of the crowd.

"Our campaign motto will be 'Every Jew a .22'. I didn't ask for mercy, I cannot compromise my principles with expediency. Some time or other, there is no other way than violence. I am not against the use of violence if necessary."

Someone in the crowd asked, "Who determines that?"

"We do," was his reply.

He announced that the JDL did not "rule out the use of dynamite if necessary." Kahane insisted it was ignorance of the law, specifically federal firearms laws relating to explosives, which got him into trouble. Next time he'd "invest $250 dollars in a stamp and be legal." In one final taunt to the legal system, he said that he planned to hold a demonstration in bomb construction for the press.

I watched much of this drama from a distance. First, from inside the United States Attorney's office, where I was being prepared for the trial, and later through the eyes of television cameras and press photos. I held no animosity toward any of these people; it just seemed to me that what they had been up to warranted more than what had amounted to a stern lecture and a fine. On the other hand, it was clear that the government had put itself in an untenable position by one of its own agencies — the FBI — whose illegal wiretap, authorized by the executive branch, short-circuited what should have been a fairly straightforward prosecution.

The situation only emboldened the JDL and its leader. Kahane continued his vocal activities with the JDL, thumbing his nose at the court. He'd show up at a JDL-sponsored meeting where armed representatives of the organization would advocate firearms ownership to those in attendance. Once, when asked by a newspaper reporter about his presence at such an event, he answered, "I'm not here," and claimed he was only at the synagogue to pray. Then he and the armed JDL member got into the same car and drove off.

Kahane became embroiled in a number of controversial incidents. Had he not been on probation, his actions would have been well protected by the Constitution's First Amendment right of freedom of speech. But he overstepped the bounds laid out for him by the sentencing judge. Often, loudly, and with gusto.

The judge demanded to know about the reports he had been given by the probation department, all indicating Kahane had flagrantly ignored the judge's orders not to have anything to do with firearms. Kahane had his story prepared. Sure, he had been at the synagogue when a JDL member was extolling the crowd to secure permits and purchase firearms. But he was in a side room, not involved in the discussion. The other man was giving him a ride to the airport. It was simply a matter of chance that he happened to be there at that moment.

The judge chose not to revoke Kahane's probation. But Kahane, his death wish never far, pushed the man. What about when he was in Israel? Were the judge's rulings valid in that country as well? Even when Kahane spoke to members of the Israeli military?

Weinstein was caught off guard. He tried to be as vague as possible in his response, telling Kahane that if he wanted to talk to Israeli troops, and the Israeli government didn't mind, then it would be up to Kahane's discretion.

The Rabbi wouldn't let it go. He again asked the judge to define what he could and could not do or say in Israel. Pushing Weinstein to the limit, the judge finally said, "All right, I will give you an answer. You may not encourage the use of weapons by anyone."

"Even in Israel?"

"Right."

"Even to the Israeli army?"

"Yes."

That last dialogue between the judge and Kahane would be sorely regretted by Kahane only a few years later. His lack of discretion would land him in a federal prison for violation of his probation for the better part of a year.[6,7]

So it was that the JDL, even after the arrest and conviction of its leader and several of its key players, was alive and well. Politically the organization was as strong, if not stronger, then ever. It would take a poorly placed incendiary device to take the life out of the JDL.

The first calls received by the New York City public safety emergency operators were frantic reports of fire and smoke on the 20th floor of the Manhattan offices of Sol Hurok. Within minutes, police units arrived. The first officers on the scene could see smoke coming from high up on the building but little else. Without firefighting gear, Nomex suites, heavy gloves and breathing apparatus, there was nothing more for the officers to do than clear traffic and pedestrians away from the possible fire location in anticipation of the soon to arrive fire units. Only in the movies can an unprotected person dare to enter such a place and come out alive. Years ago, firemen used to boast that the first people they'd have to carry out from inside a burning building would be the cops.

Once the heavily equipped fire officers got there, it was obvious that their ladder trucks were of no value in assisting them. The fire was much too high up in the building. The firemen, their breath showing in the cold January air, donned their Scott air packs (giving them twenty or so minutes of air) and made their way to the Hurok offices.

Already battling the inferno for over a quarter of an hour, those trapped on the wrong side of the flames were in a losing fight. The incendiary device, more like a bomb, really, generated so much heat that everything nearby ignited: wood, plastic, even metal.

Before the deadly fumes rendered them unconscious, some of the victims reported they could hear the banging of the fire axes as nearby doors were splintered by their rescuers. The next thing they recalled was the oxygen mask over their faces and seeing men in the soot-streaked yellow suits and the distinctive rear-brimmed hard hats working to save them. Seventeen people were pulled out of that inferno alive. One died. Iris Kones, an assistant accountant, was twenty-eight years old.

The Hurok murder had been as predictable as the outcome of a game of Russian roulette. Sooner or later, with a sufficient number of bombings, it was inevitable that someone had to die.

Cohen had purchased a hundred pounds of the necessary chemicals. Sheldon Seigel had built the devices. Sheldon Davis had instructed the four young JDL members on how to operate them, and drove with them to the sites of two places to be hit. It was Davis who would, after the devices were set off and before the JDL had become aware that a death had resulted, call in to the media reporting the incidents, ending his calls with "Never Again!"[8]

When the JDL learned of the result of their deeds, they attempted to quickly backpedal. The organization's leadership denied both knowledge of and responsibility for the act. Kahane, in Israel, called those responsible for the firebombing, "insane."

Perhaps. But he was the shepherd and it was members of his flock who had committed the crime.

At first, the NYPD only had a very strong suspicion that the bombing had been the work of the JDL. The How and the Why seemed obvious. The motive, tactics, as well as the message released to the news media shortly after the events left little doubt. What they didn't know was the Who.

Even after the arrests and the guilty pleas by Kahane and the other JDL members, bombs continued to be set off at various Soviet and Arab locations. Shots were fired into the Soviet Mission in Manhattan. The New York City Police Department continued to hold a very strong interest in the organization.

One of the two bombs used at Amtorg had failed to detonate. From that bomb's components, a Micronta timer had been salvaged, a unit commonly used for timing cakes and turkeys, available from any Radio Shack store. The detectives went out and did what detectives do. They traveled to the dozens of such stores in the NYC area, armed with photos of JDL members, and asked the clerks, "Do you recognize any of these people?"

One clerk in a Brooklyn store answered, "Yes."

On April 10th, he had sold a couple of Micronta timers and some copper wire to two of the young men in the pictures. The Amtorg bombing had taken place only a week and a half after the purchase. The photos he recognized were of Stuie Cohen and Sheldon Seigel. The receipt for the items had been filled out by one of the buyers (Seigel) using a phony name and fake address. It wasn't enough for an arrest, but at least they now knew who in the JDL had purchased these kinds of devices.

A surveillance was set up, primarily against Seigel, who was older than Cohen and therefore believed to be the more likely candidate as the actual bomb maker.

Detectives from the Arson and Explosives Unit as well as the Safe, Loft and Truck Squad did the tailing. During one of the many cat and mouse games played between the law officers and the JDL members they were following, the police got lucky. According to the detectives, Seigel and another young man, while in Seigel's old Volvo, were observed actually handling a small explosive device. In truth, as far as infernal devices went it was hardly more than a firecracker; a metal film canister loaded with gunpowder, tacks placed inside to inflict as much damage on a person as possible and a short fuse sticking out the top. But it was enough.[9,10]

Once the vehicle parked, the detectives moved in. They arrested Seigel and the other JDL members and found, inside the car, several small explosive devices, some Mace, a bayonet, and Micronta timer boxes. Seigel would later claim that all that evidence was out of sight, locked inside the vehicle's trunk, and its discovery the result of an illegal search. The detectives would state otherwise. At any rate, the car was confiscated as evidence pending the outcome of his trial on the new charges.

Seigel badly wanted his car back. Members of the Arson-Explosive squad let it be known that they'd return it to him if he cooperated with them. Seigel was very naive. And, he was desperate for that car. Not a wealthy person by any means — in fact, the majority of those involved with the JDL who I had contact with were uniform in their lack of funds — and except for mass transit, that car was his sole means of transportation.

Seigel didn't want to testify against other members in the JDL. He figured if he could just feed the Arson-Explosive detectives bits and pieces of information he'd satisfy them, get his car back, and be left alone.

His first mistake was to permit the detectives to return his car. He mistakenly believed that all he had to do was give them something in return and they'd be even. It was a foolish bargain.

According to *Chief!* by Albert Seedman, a couple of days after getting his Volvo back, Seigel called up the detective squad and said, "Listen, you know that big estate in Glen Cove the Russians bought to play around? Well, I hear some people decided to plant quite a few sticks of dynamite under the fence. It's supposed to go off today, so I hear. Now, don't say I didn't give you guys something back." ATF agents as well as members of the local police department were dispatched to the Glen Cove site. The first time they looked, they couldn't find anything. It took Seigel to visit the spot, to verify the device was there and then tell the officers its exact location.

Thus began a surreal dance between an active member of the JDL and members of the New York City Police Department. Seigel would give out bits of information, while, at the same time, remaining deeply involved within the JDL, as well as committing serious crimes with members of the organization. His main concern always remained his wish not to testify against the other JDL members. And this, he was assured time and again by the investigating detectives, as well as a United States Attorney, would not be necessary. But the promise was an empty one.

Seigel continued feeding information to the detectives, hoping that, sooner or later, it would be enough. He told of the plan to fly a radio-controlled plane (Seigel worked part-time in a model shop; although he never admitted to the detectives that it was he who had actually built the aircraft) filled with six sticks of TNT, onto the roof of the Soviet Mission in Manhattan and there to blow it up. The model flew fine. It was only Cohen's insistence on taking a turn with the plane's remote control device, and by so doing destroying the aircraft, which effectively put an end to that idea.

The second plan, had it been carried out, would have had truly international repercussions. The JDL knew that one particular member of the Soviet Mission would, at the same time each week, take his car out of the Mission's garage to visit his girlfriend. The man would spend several hours with his lover and park the vehicle on a city street. Now, although there was heavy security around the Mission, Soviet security never looked at their own cars entering the underground garage. What if the vehicle in question had several dozen sticks of dynamite, along with a timer, strapped to its undercarriage?

Finally, there was the idea to fabricate a lightweight mortar, a design obtained from the Israeli army. It would have been used to rain bombs down on the Soviet-owned estate in Glen Cove.

In return for getting back his Volvo, and with being granted immunity from prosecution, he eventually agreed to testify in a federal Grand Jury against seven JDL members involved in the Amtorg bombing. Among them were Cohen, Garfinkle, Weisel, and Bieber. In order to protect Seigel, when the arrests were made he was taken into custody as well.

But, even after the Amtorg arrests, Seigel remained highly active within the organization, to the point of making the smoke bombs which had been planted at the Hurok site.

The situation had become extraordinarily complex. It was complex for Seigel because he was a government informant and at the same time he was directly involved in a murder. It was complex for law enforcement because at first, they did not know that their informant had anything to do with the Hurok matter. And certainly, it was complex for the JDL members' defense attorneys. Unbeknownst to them, one of their clients had already testified against the other members of the organization they were representing. And, Seigel had sat in on a number of strategy sessions on how to deal with the Amtorg case.

In effect, Seigel was playing both sides against the middle. To the JDL members he was one of the boys, helping out in their plans and making the devices they wished to use. To the police, he was their inside guy, their confidential informant.

Sooner or later something had to give, and one day something did.

The Hurok case broke due to a series of seemingly unconnected events which came together. Seigel was asked by the Arson and Explosion detectives if he had any knowledge of the Hurok matter. At first, he denied the JDL was even involved in the crime.

The detectives weren't so sure. Meeting after meeting was held between the three men. The detectives, both highly experienced law officers, knew something was being kept from them. They could never have imagined what that information was. According to Seedmen, one day in early May, and by now it was months after Hurok, Seigel and the two detectives sat in a car and spoke.

"Will you still make good on that promise not to reveal me?" Seigel half asked, half begged the two men.

"For the good stuff we sure will, kid."

"Suppose I tell you who made the bomb they used at Columbia Artists Management?"

"That's the good stuff, all right."

"You swear you won't reveal me?"

"We swear, kid."

"It was me." [11]

The two law officers didn't know what to say. Here was a guy who had testified at a federal Grand Jury about a bombing he had been directly involved with. Since then, he had given the detectives information as to who had shot up the Soviet Mission to the United Nations; about plans to crash an explosives-laden radio-controlled plane on the roof of the Mission; where to find a dynamite bomb at the Glen Cove Soviet facility; and the JDL plan to plant a bomb attached to the undercarriage of a Soviet diplomat's car. And now, he told them he had helped commit a homicide — with the guy, in effect, continuing to ask, "By the way, could my name still be kept out of the matter?"

Seigel had gotten himself into an untenable position. He wanted to be protected as a government informant, give information about illegal activities and those involved in them, yet never have to testify in open court. The government had placated him at first, probably with the thought that one of the other conspirators in the various crimes would come forward and Seigel's own words would not, in fact, be needed during a trial proceeding. But the situation had gone too far, the crimes Seigel had permitted himself to become involved in too grave, for Seigel to quietly bow out now.

A long tedious and complex game began to unfold, taking place over many months. Clandestine meetings were held in unlikely places: inside tiny diners, under the West Side Highway, off country lanes. To keep the government at bay, and perhaps placate the agents so they would leave him alone, Seigel continued to give out important bits of intelligence about various JDL acts. The man only succeeded in getting himself in deeper.

During this very elaborate period of intrigue, involving perhaps half a dozen defense and prosecution attorneys and twice that number of defendants, one of the JDL attorneys, Barry Slotnick, began to suspect Seigel was not what he appeared to be. In his view, too many of the JDL's plots had been foiled for such to be the result of fortuitous chance, of the police being at just the right place and time a bit too often. Furthermore, being a very experienced criminal attorney, Slotnick was able to read the various legal papers offered by the government in a way that indicated to him that Seigel simply didn't fit into the picture of him as just another defendant.[12]

Whatever clue it was that tipped Slotnick off, he was, of course, correct. His suspicions had to be communicated to at least some of the other defense attorneys. Seigel's lawyer, Alan Dershowitz, hearing of this conjecture, finally confronted his client. It was then that he learned of Seigel's actions. He was not pleased to discover that his client was, in fact, acting as a government agent.[13]

Dershowitz's first instinct was to stop representing the young man. He had good cause to be angry and upset. A highly dedicated and professional person, he and the other lawyers in the case had spent many hours preparing for a murder case that he just now discovered had never been intended to come about against Seigel.

Dershowitz, after much soul-searching, decided to remain Seigel's attorney. One of his first acts was to disassociate himself from the other defendants in the case. Not to do so would jeopardize their rights to a fair trial. If Seigel did decide to testify, then Dershowitz, had he continued going to the other defendants' strategy sessions, might well be put in a position where he'd have to use knowledge he learned there for the benefit of his own client, to the detriment of the others. Nonetheless, Dershowitz didn't let on to the other JDL members about his client's true role in the matter. That decision would still have to be made by Seigel.

During much of this time, I had been assigned to work with Assistant United States Attorney, Joe Jaffee. We were preparing for a trial against Cohen on charges of weapons violations. If the government couldn't nail him on the heavier charges, at least it had my case to fall back on. Those crimes had taken place while Cohen was still a juvenile, so although they were serious felonies, the amount of jail time he was facing was relatively short.

I recall that one day, while going to and fro among the long corridors of the Southern District Court House, I stepped into an office. There was Seigel, sitting quietly in a chair. Not yet having decided whether he was going to testify for the government and against his friends, the man slumped where he sat, looking dejected, wan and gaunt. He raised his head when I came by and, seeing me carrying several large manila envelopes as well as some audio tapes, asked if those were "the wiretaps." I didn't understand what he was talking about. (I later learned he had meant the national security wiretaps that were to bedevil the government's case). The tapes I had with me were from the body wires I had worn during my part in the investigation as well as from the recorder I had used on my home phone. So, unsure of how to respond, I simply uttered some pleasantry and kept on going about my business.

Over the next several months, Seigel ultimately decided not to testify for the prosecution. And, because of several very technical legal matters, and his very competent attorney, not only was he able to avoid doing so, but the government was unable to put him in jail for contempt.

In the first chapter of his book, *The Best Defense*, Alan Dershowitz recounts the end of the trial:

As Cohen, Davis and Seigel were leaving the courtroom, laughing and congratulating themselves on their good fortune, Judge Bauman, aware that, for all practical purposes, those three JDL members had eluded the law after committing a most terrible crime, called after them. He asked, "Do you know who isn't in court today? Iris Kones. Someone has committed a dastardly, vicious, unforgivable, unforgettable crime; someone is frustrating the administration of justice in a case that, in my mind, involves murder. People who deliberately do so will learn the power of the law even if there are those who have literally gotten away with murder." [14]

Shortly thereafter, Cohen's trial began. The man was not represented by counsel as able as Seigel's. Prior to the actual start of the trial, I was at a meeting with the Assistant United States Attorney in the case, Joe Jaffee, and Cohen's lawyer. Because the government was charging Cohen with a narrow set of violations, none of which included the unlawful use of explosives, which had been pled to in his first federal trial, his attorney asked that the subject of bombs not be brought up. This material was especially sensitive due to the fact that the initial bombs the JDL made had been intended to be used against Blacks, and to discuss such in public would serve only to raise difficult racial issues that were not germane to the immediate trial. Joe Jaffee, a most honorable and professional man, and I agreed that the government would not bring up such matters in open court.

The defense was faced with hundreds of pages of evidence, most of which consisted of my daily reports. It was dry reading. Unlike in a novel, I had simply put down on paper who had said what to who, as well as what I had observed. I followed a strict timeline; whatever came first was written about first. Sometimes a subject that came up in one report might not surface again for many, many pages, and even then, perhaps several reports later. It was difficult reading and sometimes took considerable concentration to completely comprehend the significance of what I'd put down on paper.

I don't believe Cohen's defense attorney fully grasped these complications. Several days into the trial, while being examined by the defense, the attorney shot a question at me. He asked me why I had been at the JDL office at a certain day and hour. The reason was, I was there in preparation to go out and bomb Sonny Carson's community center. My dilemma was, if I were to testify to that, I would be in violation of our gentlemen's agreement not to talk about bombs and such.

I hemmed and hawed, attempting to respond to the question yet not touch on the matters I had pledged not to speak of in court. The attorney, thinking I was hiding something, loudly demanded of me, "Answer the question!"

Flustered, I looked over to Judge Bauman. He nodded his head and said, "You may answer the question."

With nowhere to go but the truth, I blurted out, "We were going to bomb someplace!"

The courtroom became silent. Unsure of where to go next, shuffling the copies of my reports in front of him, the attorney replied, "There's nothing in this report that says that. We agreed not to discuss such matters . . ."

I lost my temper.

"I was trying to abide by our agreement not to raise the matter of bombs and bombings. That's why I was unable to answer the question at first. But as to bombs, that's all those reports are about. My material is not a novel, it's a police report. It doesn't follow a neat order. All those reports show is who said what to whom and what I observed." Then, as a dig at the attorney, I added, "You have to read the whole set of reports to understand what's in them."

The attorney then asked for and received a recess.

When we came back into court, the defense decided, since the cat was out of the bag, it would change tactics. Now all they wanted to talk about was guns and bombs. It was a crazy defense strategy. A hundred firearms were eventually brought into the Court Room. The evidence against Cohen was so overwhelming that the man stood no chance of being acquitted on the charges. So, after a trial of several weeks, Cohen was found guilty of violating federal weapons laws.

Sentenced as a juvenile, I believe he went to prison for six months.

And, with the close of that trial, so too, did one part of life end for me. It had been a crazy time, one full of adventures not experienced by many.

I continued with the NYPD, serving as a detective for twelve years, working in various assignments: narcotics, robbery squad, homicide detective. Eventually, I rose to the rank of lieutenant, flying helicopters for the department. After twenty years with the NYPD, I decided I needed a change. I opted to become Chief of Police for a small Cape Cod town and write a few books. This one is my fourth. Life has been, and continues to be, most interesting.

The Rabbi eventually immigrated to Israel, causing quite a bit of trouble for the Israeli government. He wanted the Arabs out of the country and was not shy about voicing his opinions. He also had supporters there who had access to all the guns he needed. Unfortunately for Kahane there were none available on the day he needed a gun the most.

The JDL continued, although without Kahane at its head it went on in a much weakened form. There came a time when there was a split between the earliest members of the organization and those who took on its leadership. The acrimony went so far as to cause a court order to be issued — with Kahane's support — enjoining, among others, Cohen, Kaufman, Garfinkle and Davis from holding themselves out as the JDL.[15,16]

Kahane was cut down by an assassin's bullet while giving a speech in New York City in 1990. There were over a hundred witnesses to the crime. After a long trial his murderer was acquitted of the homicide, but the New York jury convicted him of gun possession. Only in America.

Kahane wrote, in 1974 in a *New York Times* Op-Ed article, "The United States is no longer the golden land . . . and tomorrow looms as even less golden than today."

Some people are remarkable in just how wrong they can be.

AFTERWORD

It took me some years of reflection about my involvement with the Jewish Defense League in order for me to be able and sit down and write about my assignment to that organization as an undercover New York City police officer. As a consequence, this book is not only about the JDL. It tells how the New York City Police Department responded to the threat that group posed, as well as tries to give an understanding of what it was like to be an undercover police officer, albeit from the perspective of one young, naive and very lucky man.

It should be noted that I have changed some facts in what is otherwise a true narrative. For example, I have not disclosed how to make a bomb. The names of most of the chemicals that are used in the devices I describe are fictitious. While it may be true that such information is readily available, I suggest that should you attempt to experiment along these lines, and survive, you will discover what it is like to be arrested by members of the Alcohol Tobacco and Firearms Unit. I trust you would then enjoy a stimulating relationship with the Assistant United States Attorney General assigned to prosecute you at your trial.

Likewise, some of the techniques used by the New York City Police Department's intelligence unit have either gone unmentioned or I have deliberately altered them. I have attempted, to the best of my ability, not to disseminate information that might be deemed harmful to the general public. Information is neutral; people can be irresponsible with what they do with it.

Whenever possible and appropriate I let the reader know what my views are on a given subject. Lest there be any doubt, let me say now that I believe the intelligence unit of the NYPD has done, and continues to do, a yeomen's job protecting the citizenry of that city and, indeed, the nation, from dangerous groups of social misfits. I realize that the gathering of domestic intelligence on American citizens by our law-enforcement community is controversial.

The accumulation of such information does indeed hold the potential for abuse. Yet, to preclude law officers from such activity is to invite anarchy. I hold forth no solution to the resulting conundrum. However, in regard to the NYPD, I know that the fine men and women of that department with whom I worked on this investigation comported themselves as professional law officers with the highest standards. They did their jobs with neither prejudice nor malice and with a full understanding and respect for the limitations they faced under our system of law.

Whether or not you believe the above is irrelevant to me, for what I have put down is the truth.

One last note. I have attempted to recreate conversations that took place between myself and other persons to the best of my memory and ability. While the exact wording of some dialog may have been shortened, the meaning remains faithful. Being a primary source of information, I held a number of significant advantages in my writing of this book. There were the copies I possess of my one hundred and forty two police reports. Each of these was written immediately or shortly after the incidents they describe and thus, are a most accurate reflection on past events. I also have the many pages of transcripts of the tape recordings of both the body transmitter I'd worn during this assignment as well as those generated from the recordings taken from my home telephone. Lastly, I relied on a number of additional sources for information. These included a number of books: *Chief!*, by Albert Seedman, *The Best Defense*, by Alan M. Dershowitz, *The False Prophet*, by Robert I. Friedman, and most importantly, the doctoral dissertation of Professor Shlomo Russ. Dr. Russ first approached me for an interview several years after I'd surfaced from my undercover assignment, during a time when the memories of my adventures were still quite fresh. I had numerous candid conversations with the gentleman and gave him copies of whatever documents I had in my possession in regard to the JDL investigation. Besides speaking with me, he interviewed many other members of both the law enforcement community and the JDL. His efforts and perseverance resulted in a very complete, highly detailed thousand-page dissertation on the organization, *The "Zionist Hooligans": The Jewish Defense League*. In reading his work in preparation for this book, I was both pleased and surprised to discover that I'd been quoted by Doctor Russ several times, which was most helpful in refreshing my memory concerning a number of long-forgotten incidents not put down on paper at the time. Even more importantly, he quoted extensively from his talks with members of the JDL as well. These quotes permitted me to fill in what would have otherwise been blank spaces (or worse, conjecture) in my narrative as to what transpired during a number of critical incidents.

I would like the reader to note that this work is the result of a healthy struggle between my editor, Ira Wood, and myself. I had a tendency, when putting my thoughts on paper about my time as an undercover police officer, to write as if I were still wording this project for one of my police reports. Ira would have none of it. He either made me convert long boring sections of verbatim transcript conversation into paragraph-size prose or otherwise greatly reduce my repetitive verbiage. When I would write down every nuance about the firearms I was handling, he had me rewrite the material so that a layman would be comfortable with the language.

One of the biggest problems I had was putting on paper an interesting narrative of the proceedings while maintaining the accuracy of the work. Life is messy. Actual timelines of events are often hard to relate in a way that doesn't put a reader to sleep. I have been faithful to the truth, but by necessity found I had to insert some of the events a bit out of their proper time frames. To have done otherwise would have made this work much less interesting and far more difficult to follow.

The actual names of those involved were used whenever possible. However, lawyers rule. Prudence — and good taste — required pseudonyms to be used for certain individuals in the narrative. The decisions were made by following these guidelines: Many of those involved in the JDL were upstanding citizens who committed no violations of law. It would hardly be fair to name them in this book. Some members of the organization did do foolish things. But, since events recounted in this book took place some 30 years ago, when I was a rookie cop in my twenties, and many of the Jewish Defense League members were still in their teens and twenties, I have decided that it would serve no purpose to use the actual names of the JDL members — whose lives, in many cases, may have gone in very different directions in the years since these events took place. Therefore, I have changed the names of the JDL members and their associates with the exception of the group's leader, Rabbi Meir Kahane, and the handful of other JDL members who were charged with and tried for, convicted of, or pleaded guilty to, crimes related to their JDL activities.

ACKNOWLEDGEMENTS AND SOURCES

A number of newspapers as well as four very fine books were consulted for Chapter Twenty-One:

The New York Times, The New York Daily News, The Long Island Press.

Shlomo Mordechai Russ, *The "Zionist Hooligans": The Jewish Defense League*, City University of New York, 1981.

Alan M. Dershowitz, *The Best Defense*, Vintage Books, Random House, New York, 1982.

Albert A. Seedman, *Chief!*, Arthur Fields Books, Inc., New York, 1974.

Robert I. Friedman, *The False Prophet*, Lawrence Hill Books, Brooklyn, New York, 1990.

[1]Russ, p. 470
[2]Russ, p. 488
[3]Dershowitz, p. 38
[4]Russ, p. 510
[5]Russ, pp. 508-509
[6]Russ, p. 538
[7]Friedman, p.180
[8]Russ, pp. 554-556
[9]Seedman, p. 280
[10]Dershowitz, p. 25
[11]Seedman, p. 312
[12]Russ, p. 556
[13]Dershowitz, p. 21
[14]Dershowitz, p. 78
[15]Russ, p. 1,046
[16]Friedman, p. 176

THE AUTHOR

Before becoming Chief of Police of the Cape Cod fishing village of Wellfleet, Massachusetts, Richard Rosenthal spent twenty years in the New York City Police Department, where he ran the Heavy Weapons and Undercover Weapons Training programs and, as a detective, dealt with homicide, narcotics, and armed robbery. Before joining the NYPD, he worked for U.S. Air Force military intelligence as a Russian language specialist. Pocket Books published his two popular books of police craft, *Sky Cops* and *K-9 Cops*, as well as his novel, *The Murder of Old Comrades*, "A spicy police procedural about KGB assassins on the loose in Manhattan," according to *The Wall Street Journal*, which "put Mr. Rosenthal on the map in big-league publishing."